ARCHAEOLOGICAL SITES OF DI

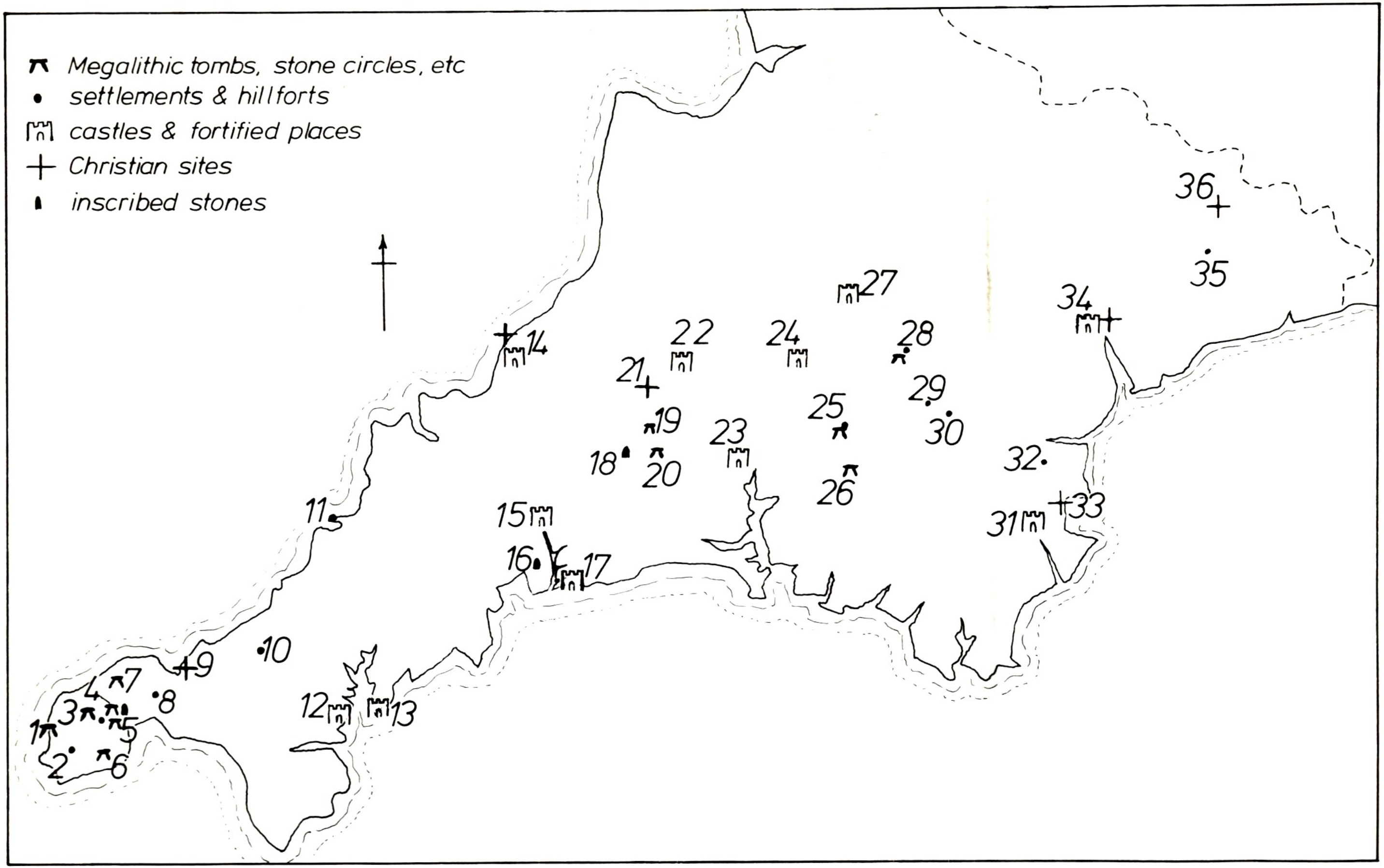
Megalithic tombs, stone circles, etc
settlements & hillforts
castles & fortified places
Christian sites
inscribed stones
1
2
3
4
5
6
7
8
9
10
11
12
13
14
15
16
17
18
19
20
21
22
23
24
25
26
27
28
29
30
31
32
33
34
35
36

# ARCHAEOLOGICAL SITES OF DEVON and CORNWALL

T. Clare

MOORLAND PUBLISHING

ISBN 0 86190 057 X (hardback)
ISBN 0 86190 058 8 (paperback)

To Halina and Andrew



Printed in Great Britain by
Butler & Tanner Ltd, Frome
Moorland Publishing Co Ltd,
PO Box 2, 9-11 Station Street,
Ashbourne, Derbyshire,
DE6 1DZ.

# Contents

# Preface

This is a guide to both individual sites and the principal types of monument. The sites are arranged geographically (see map) but there is also a discussion of the principal categories.

The chosen sites are good examples of their type and have either public access or are adjacent to public rights of way. In the latter case, eg Hembury, it would be courteous to seek permission from the farmer of you wish to leave the footpath. All sites are ancient monuments and as such it is an offence to deface, disturb or damage them in any way. Equally the country code should be followed.

> Each site has a ground plan marked with one or more viewpoints. These refer to the corresponding illustrations and show the features of special interest which may be seen from that spot, and their significance is explained in the accompanying notes.

# Acknowledgements

The author wishes to thank the British Museum and Exeter City Council for permission to use manuscripts as the base for some illustrations. Thanks are also due to all who read and commented upon the text: J. Cox, T. Greeves, J. Hughes, N. Johnston, H. Slade and S. Timms — although final responsibility for interpretation is the author's.

Sources of drawings:

The plans reproduced in this book are based on the following: Page 21 (Trethurgy Round): *Cornish Arch*, **12**, p 27; page 26 (Croft Moraig): *PPS*, **37**, plate 1a; page 7: D. N. Riley, *Early Landscape from the Air*, (Sheffield, 1980); page 9 (Durrington Walls): G. J. Wainwright, *Durrington Walls*, (London 1971), fig 17; page 15: *PPS*, **44**, p313; p19: *Arch*, **76**, fig 3; page 30: *Arch*, **83**, plate LXII; page 48: BM Ms Cotton Aug I, 43; page 87: *Arch J*, **130**, p257; page 105: plan by J. Allen; page 125: plan by H. Slade; page 130: *Proc Devon Arch Expl Soc*, **4**, p30; page 34 (Exeter Bridge): unknown artist, Devon Local History Library; page 145 (Exeter Common Seal): Devon County Record Office.

Abbreviations

*Arch*: Archaeologia
*Arch J*: Archaeological Journal
*PPS*: Proceedings of Prehistoric Society

# Introduction: Sites and Landscapes

In the previous volume in this series, *Archaeological Sites of the Lake District*, the monuments were arranged by type, eg stone circles, settlements, Roman forts, castles, monasteries, etc, for that is the easiest method of study, but such a system becomes difficult to operate at places like Merrivale and Kestor on Dartmoor. There, 'stone circles' and settlement remains exist side by side or superimposed in a palimpsest. While it is still possible to identify the different types of monument within such palimpsests, the relationship of individual remains to each other must first be explored before they are extracted for study by type. Here, then, the sites are arranged by location from west to east, with a separate discussion of them as examples of a particular type.

The people who divided the land and built their huts at Merrivale and Kestor, did so amongst earlier man-made features like the stone rows. The rows were part of the contemporary environment, either mere curiosities which could be built over, quarried or adapted for new uses, or places of superstitious dread which should not be touched. In either case to fully understand the settlement remains requires an awareness and discussion of the stone rows, and vice versa.

For those charged with protecting our heritage the question is, should such ancient or fossil landscapes be protected as a whole or is it sufficient merely to protect the individual walls and standing stones? The problem is best seen at Grimspound. Although contemporary with Kestor it has no extensive 'field system' around it. The reason for the difference has to be explained and thus the blank area is as relevant to future study as the protected walls.

Archaeological sites must, therefore, be considered in geographical and chronological context. In many cases, however, the ancient landscape around a monument has been destroyed. At Hembury it can be glimpsed in the banks on the sides and at the bottom of the hill, at Dunkeswell in the earthworks beyond the present buildings and at St Buryan in the concentration of 'sites'. Elsewhere the context might now be detected only as crop marks or by infra-red photography.

However, because landscapes are palimpsests of features of differing age it is never possible to point to a landscape as being wholly of one period. The Roman landscape included all the prehistoric features still surviving and many more now lost. William the Conqueror utilised the Roman defences at Exeter, while a medieval farmer at Hound Tor rebuilt a prehistoric farmstead for his own use. Yet in some instances a landscape has been 'frozen' in time by the retreat of intensive farming. The ancient landscape preserved at Kestor, Hound Tor and elsewhere, date to the time when the fields and farms were last utilised, not when they were first built. The modern landscape is dated by the new road or bungalow not by the adjacent sixteenth-century cottage.

On the other hand if a typical portion of twentieth-century landscape were to be preserved such a cottage would have to be included even though it 'dated' to a different period. In this book, as in that on the Lake District, the sites are divided into types on the basis of their function rather than on their date.

Where intensive farming has not retreated, the ancient elements of the landscape are isolated as individual 'sites'. Sometimes they are left in the corner of a field, like Trethevy Quoit, or partly used for existing field boundaries, eg Carn Euny **8**. Elsewhere modern field boundaries may perpetuate ancient land divisions which have long since disap-

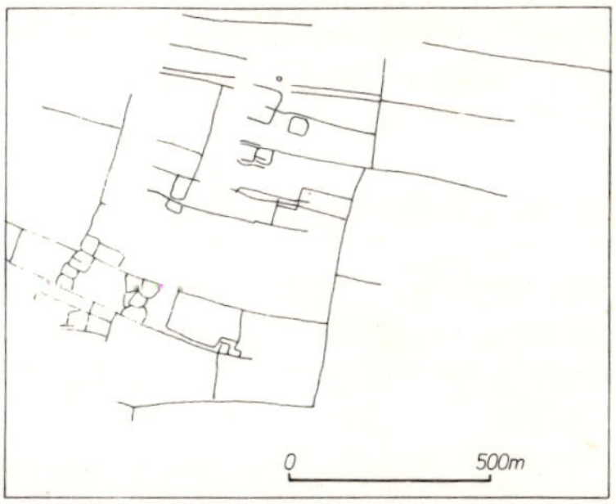


*Crop marks at Babworth, Notts: a landscape analogous to that surviving at Kestor*

peared. The administrative divisions of Cornwall for example are probably the administrative units of Roman and post-Roman times. How they relate if at all, to the small kingdoms attested by the Men Scryfa and Tristan stones is not clear, but by analogy with Wales there should have existed units of land known as 'multiple estates'. Such units embraced different kinds of land just as the reave did at Merrivale a thousand years before the Romans. Multiple estates in the legal sense of medieval Wales may not have existed in pre-Roman times but there were almost certainly areas of land functioning in a similar way.

By Roman times there was a well established network of lanes and tracks (Chysauster, Carn Euny and Milber Down) and a hierachy of settlement: large hillforts like Hembury, smaller centres like Restormel **1** or Milber Down and individual farms such as Kestor **1** or Hound Tor **5**. In the post-Roman period a similar hierachy can be recognised and alongside places like Chun Castle and Exeter were the graveyards such as Lewannick and Phillack. Norman castles were usually built in or near such centres and if a town did not exist there, growth was encouraged, as at Launceston.

What we recognise as archaeological sites were thus once part of functioning communities, economies and landscapes, from which our own is directly descended. Such sites have been fortuitously preserved because the margin of enclosed land left them beyond later enclosure or because land usage has not required them to be swept away. It follows their survival is dependent upon no change in existing use.

# Types of Site

## Megalithic Tombs, Circles and Kindred Monuments

(Sites 1, 3, 4, 5, 6, 7, 11, 19, 20, 25, 26, 28)
Three principal types of *megalithic tomb* can be recognised: those with an antechamber (Zennor and Trethevy), those with a simple box-like chamber enclosed by a mound (Chun) and those with a low rectangular chamber at the edge of a mound (Tregiffian at St Buryan, Carn Gluze and Pennance at SW448376). Lanyon is too ruined to be classified. All three types appear to be broadly contemporary and to share the same ritual traditions; pits, for example, are recorded at Zennor, Tregiffian, Carn Gluze and Lanyon (the character of Trethevy is not adequately recorded). Such features, together with evidence from sites elsewhere, suggest chambered tombs were not solely funerary, although the rituals might involve mortuary material. The focus for the rituals was either the chamber or its entrance. At Zennor, for example, the Bronze Age material had been buried in the antechamber and at Chun, where the chamber was enveloped by its mound, there appears to have been a false portal. Again, the stones at Tregiffian were decorated, the most elaborate one being by the entrance. That stone was, however, hidden by the kerb, an act which recalls the hidden structure at Carn Gluze. There too, however, the chamber, at the edge of the mound and on the axis of the pit sealed by that mound, could be the focus for continued ritual.

*Pennance*

The Carn Gluze type of chamber is aptly called an *entrance grave* while the Trethevy type is known in Wales and Ireland as a *portal dolmen*. Interestingly the portal dolmen at Dyffryn Ardudwy near Harlech contained a stone pendant similar to the 'whetstone' from Zennor. The Dyffryn site contained both Neolithic and Bronze Age material and the implication there and elsewhere is that the chambers could have been open for centuries prior to them being sealed (perhaps in the Bronze Age). Thus with the possible exception of Carn Gluze the Bronze Age material from the Cornish megalithic tombs probably represents a final rather than a primary deposit.

By the late-Neolithic, however, another type of complex ritual site had developed — the *henge*, a late example of which is Castilly (SX031629). The *henge* was a circular, embanked enclosure containing pits, stones, posts or complex circular timber buildings. Some of the latter, like the facades of some tombs, were approached by rows or avenues of posts. From the latter are surely developed the *stone rows* of Dartmoor, their termini developed from the various foci of Neolithic ritual: the blocking stone, flanking stones, the mound or circular area.

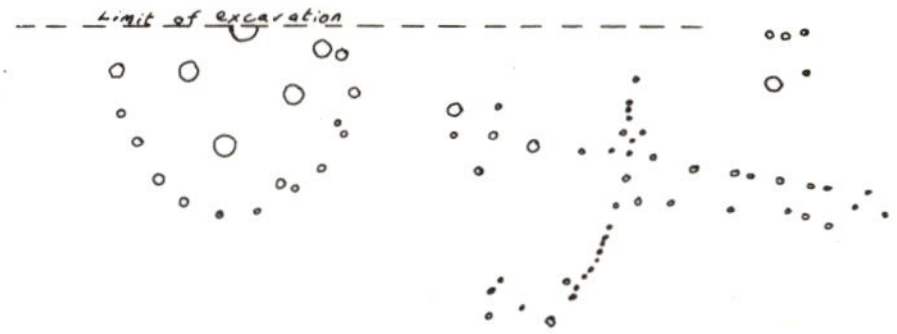


*Arrangement of timbers in the North Circle at Durrington Walls (henge)*

The (other) Early Bronze Age ritual sites show, not surprisingly, only variations on a basic theme or themes: plain, large diameter circles (the Merry Maidens at St Buryans, the Hurlers, Merrivale **12** and Ringmoor Down **1**), circles with mounds in the middle (Ringmoor Down **3**), mounds with circles around the base (Merrivale **8** and Ringmoor Down **2**), mounds covering circles (Shovel Down **9H**), mounds sealing circular embanked areas (Ringmoor Down **4**), circular banks enclosing mounds (Merrivale **10**).

The reason for one type of monument as opposed to another is not often apparent, but available building materials may have been a factor. Another factor seems to be culture/tradition. *Stone rows*, for example, are concentrated on Dartmoor, while the *entrance grave* seems to be confined to West Cornwall.

**Settlements and Hillforts**

(Sites, 2, 3, 8, 10, 11, 24, 25, 28, 29, 30, 32, 34 and 35)

The earliest permanent settlements belong to the Neolithic and two types may be recognised:

*Castilly*

the isolated farmstead, no example of which is visible, and hilltop enclosures like Carn Brea and Hembury in their earliest phases. The differences between the two types may reflect a hierachy of settlement with the hilltop enclosures serving, perhaps, as focal points and religious centres.

By Early Bronze Age times the rectangular (early Neolithic) building had given way to the tradition of building circular structures. Again two types may be recognised: the unenclosed hut like Merrivale **3** and those grouped loosely within enclosures, such as Grimspound and perhaps Merrivale **2**. Elsewhere defended hilltop enclosures have been shown to develop in the late Bronze Age and evidence of activity at that time has been found at Carn Brea. Like the Neolithic hilltop enclosures the later prehistoric hillforts may have had a ritual element. A deep shaft with votive deposits was, for example, found inside the hillfort at Cadbury (SX913052, not included here) while the bronzes from Milber Down may also have been votive. Similarly the settlement at Carn Euny seems to have had provision for ritual in the form of the fogou. It is reasonable to infer that prehistoric man, like most since, did not readily separate religion and everyday living.

The defences of the 'hillforts' vary from the glacis at Hembury to the well constructed walls of Chun, and the ramparts can be massed, again as at Hembury, or widely spaced like Milber Down, Restormel **1**, Trevelgue and perhaps Chun. Such differences must reflect function as well as the cultural influences and traditions of the builders. Not surprisingly, therefore, some sites exhibit a mixture of features rather than belonging to one of the specific types recognised by archaeologists.

Trevelgue, for example, is a headland defended by both widely spaced ramparts and ones massed together. Perhaps it is of two periods with the wide spacing being the earlier form, but if so defended promontories were not solely the work of late prehistoric immigrants as sometimes claimed. Some hillforts such as Chun and Castle Dore (SX 103548) were refurbished or continued in the post-Roman period serving, as they probably had in prehistoric times, as the centres of lordship.

The lesser settlements of the late Iron Age seem to have been enclosed sites, eg Kestor **1** and Hound Tor **5**. A specific type of enclosed settlement was the *Round* — a small circular or oval enclosure with a single rampart and ditch. The origin of the type is not clear, but as several overlie Bronze Age settlements it is probable they evolved from existing types such as Grimspound. *Rounds* continued into the Roman period, although some assumed rectilinear form as at Trevinnick (SX 008787) and Trevelgue **4**.

A regional type partly contemporary with the *Round* was the *courtyard house* (Chysauster and Carn Euny). The type is confined to Penwith and may reflect foreign influence. A number were built within *Rounds* and both at Chysauster and Carn Euny the more traditional round hut was present.

Post-Roman settlement types are difficult to identify, partly because of the lack of pottery in use at that time and partly because many probably lie beneath or near their later or modern successors. The place name element *Tref* is widely held to denote such farms (the element *Caer* apparently being used of *Rounds*). Then, as for the previous four thousand years, the overall settlement pattern was one of dispersed farmsteads. It was the Romans at Exeter and later the Saxons at Lydford who planted towns; a policy continued in later medieval times at Launceston, Okehampton and elsewhere.

## Castles and fortified buildings

(Sites, 12, 13, 14, 15, 17, 22, 23, 24, 27, 31, and 34)

Although by 1066 there were several fortified towns like Exeter and Lydford, there were no castles. The earliest examples, built by the Normans, were of earth and timber with occasionally one part in stone — the gatehouse at Exeter and Restormel and a tower at Okehampton. Three types of early castle can be recognised: the ringwork (Lydford **8**) the ringwork and bailey (Exeter and Restormel) and the motte and bailey (Launceston, Okehampton and Lydford in its later form).

The ringworks do not seem to have possessed residential towers which could be called keeps. The earliest keeps, square in plan, occur at Okehampton and Totnes. At the latter site it was replaced by a shell keep similar to that of Launceston, while at Lydford the form of a great keep was adopted for the twelfth-century prison, even to the point of later being given a bogus motte. At Tintagel the headland seems to have functioned like a ringwork and there was no keep, while the walls of the shell keep at Plympton (SX 543558) can be seen to have been reinforced with horizontal timbers.

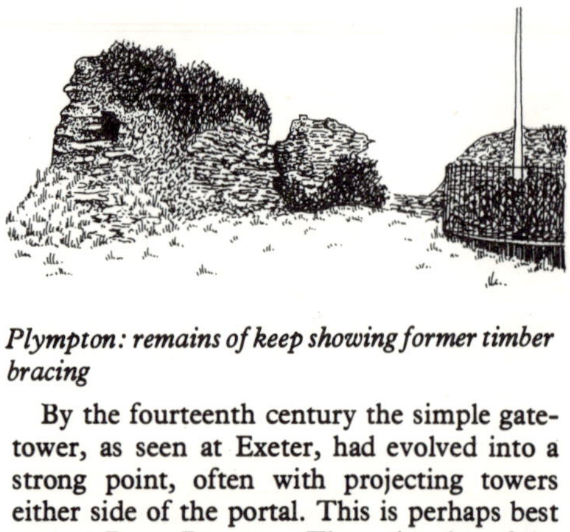

*Plympton: remains of keep showing former timber bracing*

By the fourteenth century the simple gatetower, as seen at Exeter, had evolved into a strong point, often with projecting towers either side of the portal. This is perhaps best seen at Berry Pomeroy. There the plan of the castle is very similar to many contemporary smaller castles, eg Tiverton and Hemyock. Rectilinear in plan, they were moated and had a tower at each corner and a gatetower in the centre of one side. Berry Pomeroy does not conform exactly, for its gatetower is in one corner and there is no full moat: differences which may reflect the topography.

Berry Pomeroy also seems to have had an inner court emphasising that, like all castles, it was primarily a residence, albeit a fortified one. Its translation into a palace as intended by Seymour was not, therefore, wholly inappropriate. Nor is it surprising to find the arrangement of Tiverton or Berry Pomeroy echoed in the houses of the wealthy a century later, as at Cotehele. There the functions of the building, and its general ancestor the 'castle', as a residence and centre of an estate can be readily appreciated.

By the time Cotehele was built the need for the wealthy to live within a well fortified building had passed. At about the same time, however, there was increasing Royal activity with the construction of a series of new 'castles' along the south coast. Built for cannon, their gun portals are very unlike the small, earlier ones at Berry Pomeroy, Cotehele and Fowey. By the time of Cotehele, Pendennis and St Mawes the defence of the realm had moved away from the feudal system to one under the direct control of Central Government.

**Christian Sites**

(Sites, 9, 14, 21, 33, 34 and 36)

Christianity reached Britain in Roman times, but was apparently extinguished in most of what is now England by the arrival of pagan Angles and Saxons. The church survived and developed, however, amongst the remaining British or Celtic population. The physical evidence for continuity can be seen in the Chi Rho monogram at Phillack and, perhaps, in the circular graveyards there and at Lewannick which echo, if not draw upon, the pre-Roman traditions of circular ritual enclosures. In the medieval *Life Of Kentigern* the saint travels to what is now Glasgow and makes the first burial in a circular cemetery previously 'consecrated' by Ninian. The bier was a waggon pulled by two untamed bulls and the cemetery is described as a grove of trees. The single, initial burial in the Kentigern story recalls the 'Memoria' stone from Lewannick, which may have been erected by a similar 'primary' grave.

Kentigern, like the other contemporary saints was a monk, but a monk in the tradition of the early church — a solitary or hermit. Monasticism developed when groups of hermits joined together for certain practices, eg church on Sunday and special meals, and the tradition reached Britain before the major dislocation of contact with the continent about AD 470. After that the idea developed amongst the 'Celtic' population and the early remains at Tintagel seem to belong to such an establishment. The disruption of contact, however, cut off the 'Celtic Church' from new ideas and in particular those of St Benedict. Born about AD 480 he became head of a monastery of the old type and 'reformed' it by the adoption of a set of rules.

From that reform, introduced into England with St Augustine, came the almost stereotyped medieval monastery as seen, for example, at Torre Abbey. The church **A** was of primary importance. As some services were held at night the dormitory **B** was immediately adjacent, a staircase **C** linking the two. A staircase **D** gave daytime access to the cloisters **E** which were for meditation and literary work.

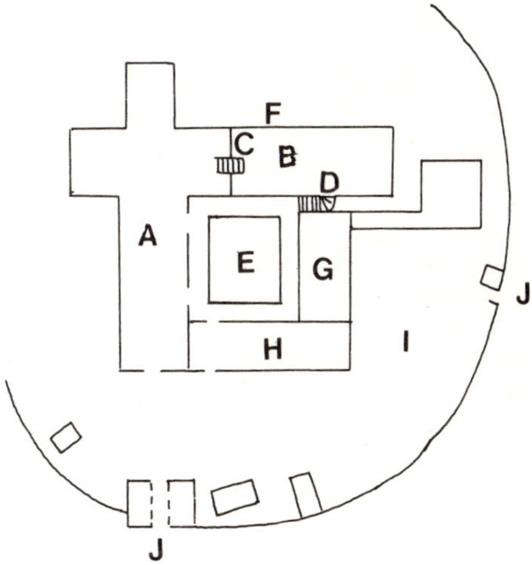


As maximum light was thus required the cloisters were built to the south of the church. On the eastern side, beneath the dormitory, was the chapterhouse **F** and to the south the refectory **G**. The western range **H** might be used for guests or the abbot, as at Torre Abbey, or in the case of the Cistercians for lay brethren as at Dunkeswell. Beyond the conventual buildings was an outer-court **I** entered through gatehouses **J**, like those at Dunkeswell and Torre Abbey. Travellers would be accommodated in or near the gatehouses while within the court or immediately outside were farm buildings. An important element in the monastic diet was fish, two large ponds surviving at Dunkeswell. The monasteries were thus the centres of estates and farmland with orchards, gardens and meadows. After the dissolution the estates were taken by lay owners who in a few instances, eg Torre Abbey, converted the buildings for their own use.

**Crosses and Inscribed Stones**

(Sites 4, 16, 18 and 21)

Their importance lies in the insight they give to the character and structure of the population in the centuries after the Roman withdrawal. Stones with Irish names or the Ogham script, as at Lewannick, attest the presence of the immigrants in the fifth century AD. Such settlement would seem to have followed the Irish raiding of the Severn coast from at least AD 260 onwards. What protective measures the Romans took have never been explored. It is conceivable, bearing in mind the (later) attested settlement and the traditions concerning one Cairpre of Kerry, that the Romans settled some Irish chiefs and their warbands as *foederati*, rather like some Saxons were employed to repulse their fellow countrymen.

On the evidence of Men Scryfa and the Tristan Stone the fifth/sixth-century Britons were organised under a number of petty kings or lords, presumably based in nearby fortifications like Chun Castle or Castle Dore. There was also an overking for Gildas' invective names Constantine of Dumnonia. Like Cairpre of Kerry such kings were able to lead their followers to settle overseas and that is what some of the Britons did in Britanny in the fifth and sixth centuries. Riwal, a 'chief of Dumnonia', was one such king and was known to the Romans as Pomperius Regalis.

In the seventh century the Saxons penetrated Devon in a series of battles, in 614, 658 and 682. Only west of the Tamar did the British maintain their political independence. The Doniert Stone carries the name of one such king and the present name of the area 'Cornwall' is derived from *Cornwealas* meaning the Welsh (*Walas*) in the old tribal area of the *Cornovii*. The *Cornovii* seem to have been a separate 'tribal' grouping within the larger (Roman) political unit of Dumnonia.

In the ninth and tenth centuries the area was subject to new, if indirect, Irish influence through Scandinavian raiders. To them or their imitators belong the 'hogback' stone in Lanivet churchyard (SX 039642) and the Cardinham Cross (SX 123687). In 838 the British/Welsh in 'Cornwall' combined with the Scandinavian raiders against the Saxons. They were defeated by Eadgar and the victory followed up by Athelstan. In 926 Athelstan expelled the British from Exeter and Huwal, King of Cornwall, submitted to the Saxon kings.

*Hogback* **A** *and cross* **B** *at Lanivet*

# 1 Carn Gluze
SW 353315

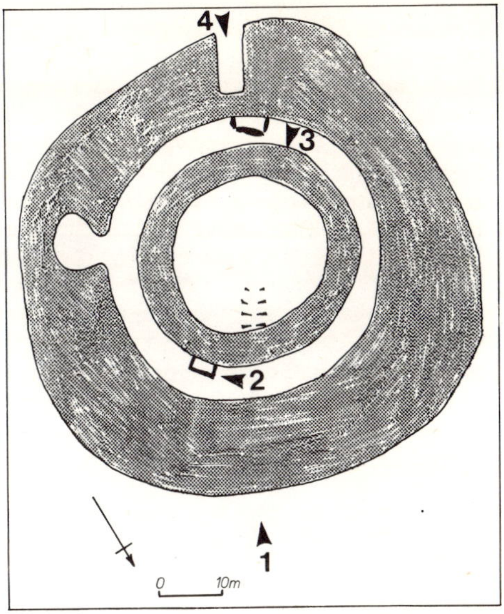


Until the middle of the nineteenth century the site was covered by mining debris similar to that still on the other side of the road. The excavation or 'process of overhauling the mound' revealed a large cairn with a walled exterior **A**. The cairn was found to conceal another walled structure **B**. The purposeful 'hiding' of walls is a feature of Neolithic monuments as well as Bronze Age ones, and the circular structure **B** may also best be paralleled in Stone Age sites like Ty Isaf (Brecknock). Whether wall **A** was itself deliberately hidden cannot now be determined, but its upper part may have been visible in medieval times if **C**, not described by the excavator, is a kiln of that period.

▼

1

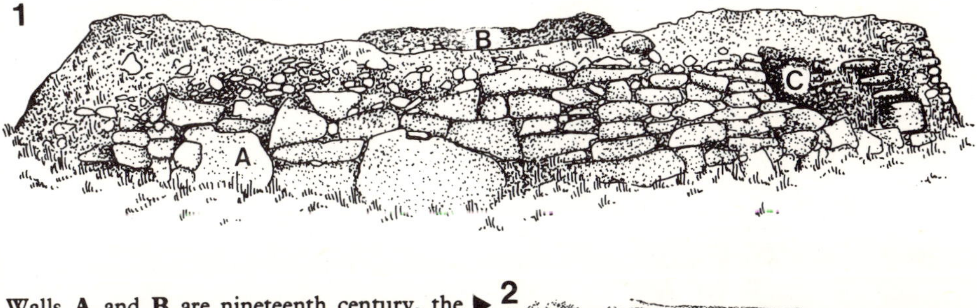


Walls **A** and **B** are nineteenth century, the cairn retained by wall **1A** originally extended to and covered a large pit at **C** and cist **D**. The latter which had contained some article of wood was built against the wall **E** of the inner structure **1B**. A short distance inside wall **E** was a second, concentric wall also with a markedly curved surface. The stones between were found to be 'aslant' suggesting **E** was the retaining wall for carefully pitched slabs laid against the hidden wall. Such a method of building is again paralleled in Neolithic tombs and in particular in the material blocking the entrances. The structure here, however, is dated to the Bronze Age by urns found within a number of cists formerly at **F**. Earlier than the cists was the pit **C** entered by trench **G**. The pit which was 7 ft (2·1m) below ground and

▶ 2

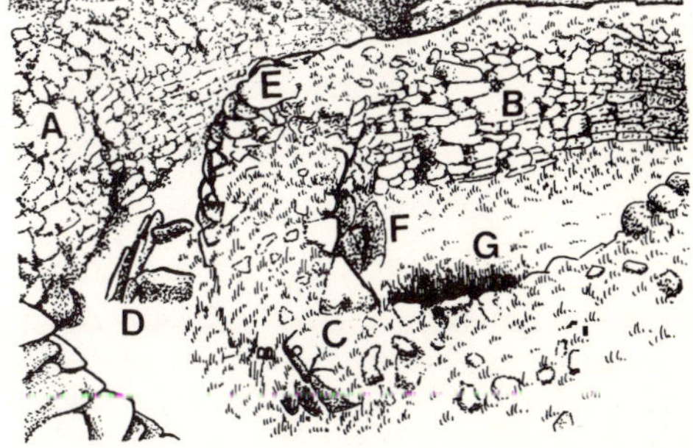


'hollowed out like a cave under hard soil' contained greasy mould and a bead. The mould suggests vegetable material, perhaps a ritual offering of 'fruits of the earth'.

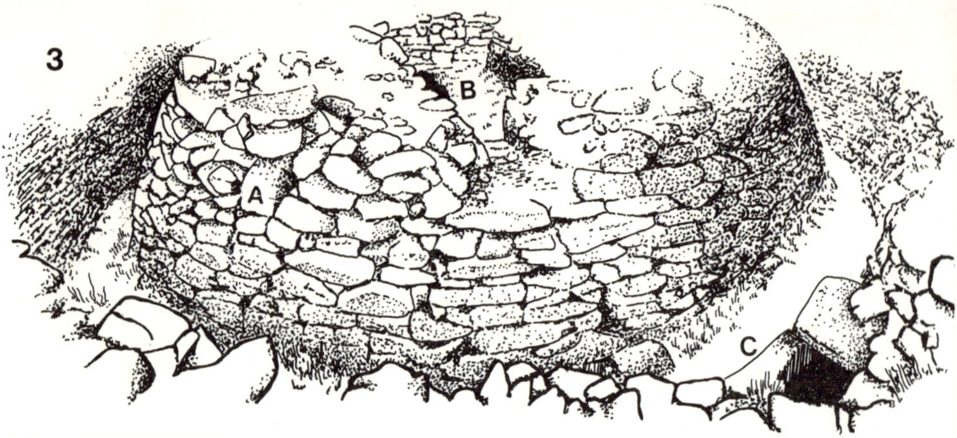


▲

The overall shape of the buried inner structure represented by wall **A** and the other hidden wall cannot now be determined, but its markedly curved surface suggests a dome. It had been built on a surface of 'ashes and charred wood' and must have been contemporary with the Bronze Age cists at **B**. Nothing was found in cist **C**, but its short axis is almost exactly that of **2D** suggesting deliberate alignment. Such a line would have passed close to several of the cists at **B** implying that **C** and **2D** were built by the same people, ie the whole structure was built at one time.

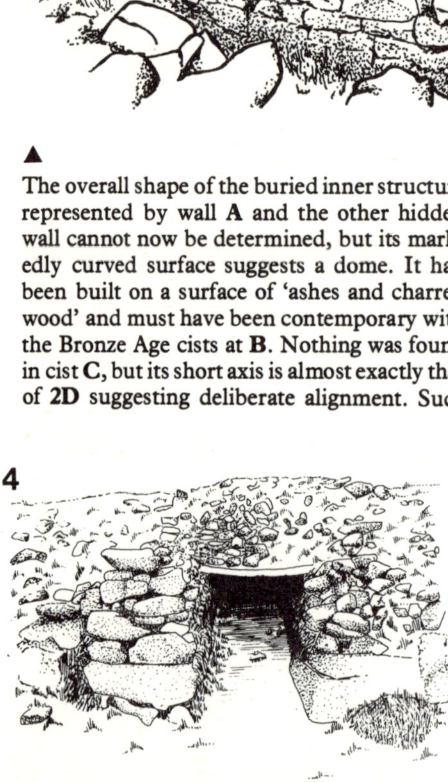


◀

Interestingly, therefore, the long axis of this chamber is approximately that of the inner pit **2C** and different from that of the cists. The chamber appears to be an example of the type of Megalithic tomb found at Tregiffian (St Buryan) and the burnt human bones and pottery beneath its paved floor can be paralleled in such sites. There, and elsewhere, the chamber is suspected of being a Neolithic structure with the associated Bronze Age material representing merely the final use prior to sealing. If that were the case here the difference in orientation between the pit and chamber on the one hand and the Bronze Age cists on the other would be explained, but the chamber would have needed to be supported by its own mound. Such a feature may have existed here for the excavator drew attention to a 'curious bulge' in the final cairn. On balance, however, it seems easiest to regard the present cairn and chamber as being of one period, and to find parallels in a number of Bronze Age ring cairns where some of the perimeter stones are arranged like the entrance of a chambered tomb. Such circular sites seem to have stood open for some time prior to their being sealed by a mound, and the two pits and cists imply the cairn here also sealed an area previously set aside for ritual. How long that area remained open prior to sealing is unclear.

*An area was chosen for ritual and within that area two pits were dug. One at least contained offerings of the fruits of the earth. The area was subsequently sealed by a walled dome which was hidden by a larger cairn. Although Bronze Age in date, the construction and practices betray continuity with those of the Neolithic.*

**2 Carn Euny**
SW 402288

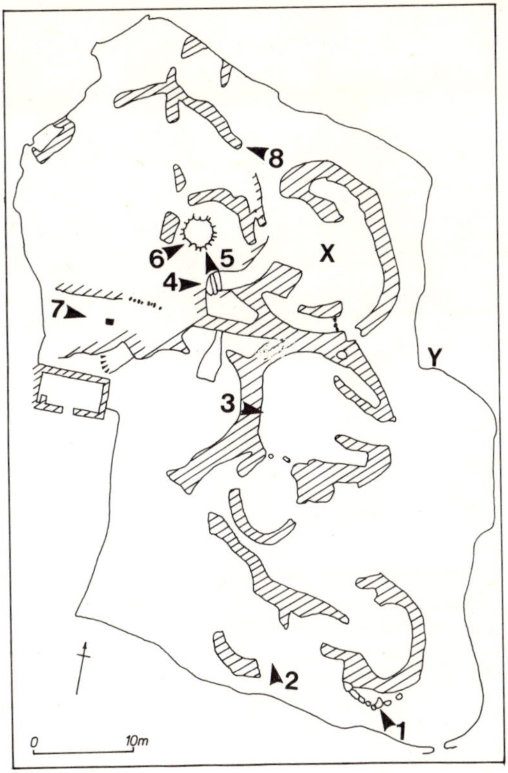


The remains consist of a number of buildings or houses not all of which are contemporary. House **A** and area **B**, for example, were built over the site of a circular timber house and, later, a ditch dug through them.

▼

1

2

▲
This hut, once more complete, contains a padstone **A** for a post. It is generally assumed the purpose of such a post was to support the roof, although such an upright would not be necessary if the building was of small diameter and the rafters secured at the wall top (see Merrivale **3**). It is significant, therefore, that **A** is not central. As the centre of the building was destroyed by a later ditch the padstone must be in its original position — unless moved prior to digging of the ditch.

3

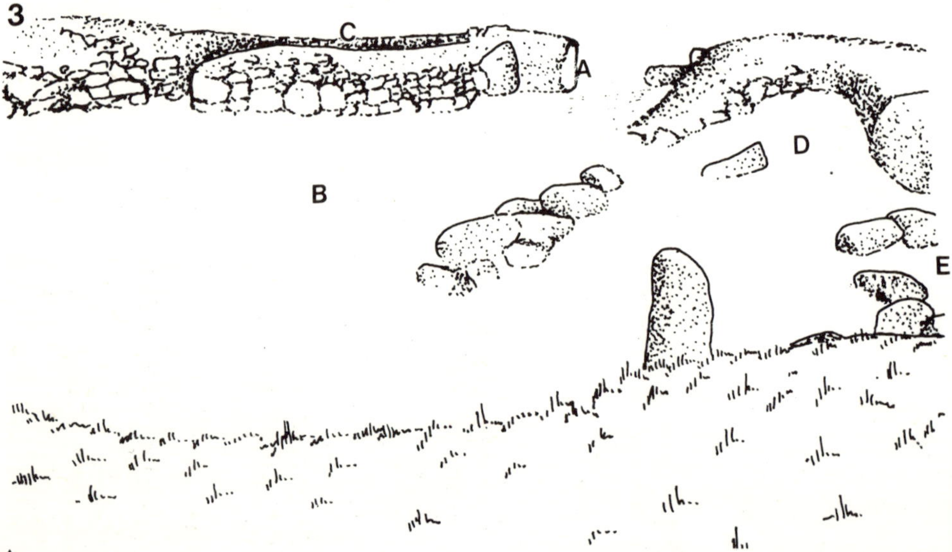


▲
The earlier hut beneath this house seems to have been roofed with thatch for a layer of black, greasy material overlay its floor. The visible structure appears to be a 'courtyard house' like Chysauster **2**. Its door, flanked by jambs **A**, led into a courtyard **B** on either side of which was a long room **C** and **D**. There is, however, no evidence for a separate domestic area as at Chysauster, unless it is the hut at **E**. That is unlikely as **E** was built later and associated with Roman pottery. In the absence of an identifiable 'domestic area' could the courtyard have been roofed and lived in? The width of the door at **A** would make it very draughty but signs of occupation were found in **D**.

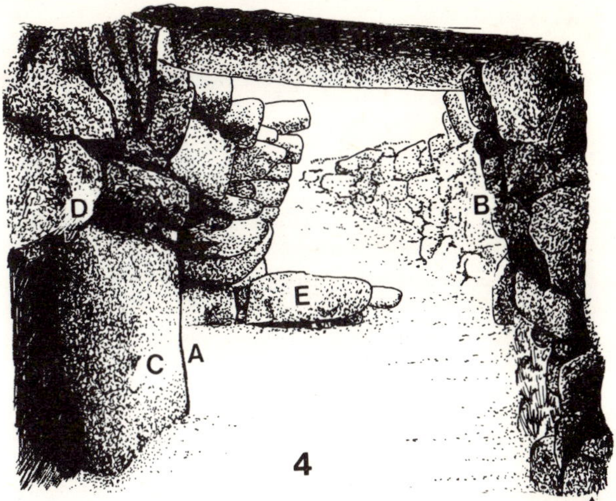


▲

The 'courtyard house' at **X** on the plan overlies and is, therefore, later than this passage or fogou which is itself of two periods. The passage cut an earlier one **A** and **B** at right angles. At the corner of the two the later builders had to prop and wedge the roof with a separate slab **C** and stones **D**. Later still the new passage was blocked at **E**. Charcoal, including hazel and gorse, from beneath the floor gave a radiocarbon date for the passage of 130 ± 80 bc.

The first passage led into the circular chamber. A pit had been dug in the centre of its floor and on the opposite side to the passage was a recess **A**, both of unknown purpose.

▼

▲ Although the upper part of the chamber **A** is corbelled it probably never stood much higher. If there was a roof it was of timber or thatch. The purpose of the chamber is unknown and it has no known parallels unless the fogou at Gulegullas is related. It was dug in the eighteenth century and said to have had a room with two niches. Borlase found pits in two of the other fogous he excavated and one was filled with ashes. The pits and chambers echo the earlier megaliths and imply a non-utilitarian function for chamber and fogou. Both were built by constructing the walls in a trench and then backfilling. How long **A** remained open is uncertain but hut **B** was later built over the top for its occupation debris ran over stones **C**. By the time of hut **B**, therefore, unless the chamber continued to serve its original purpose it must have been filled in or boarded over.

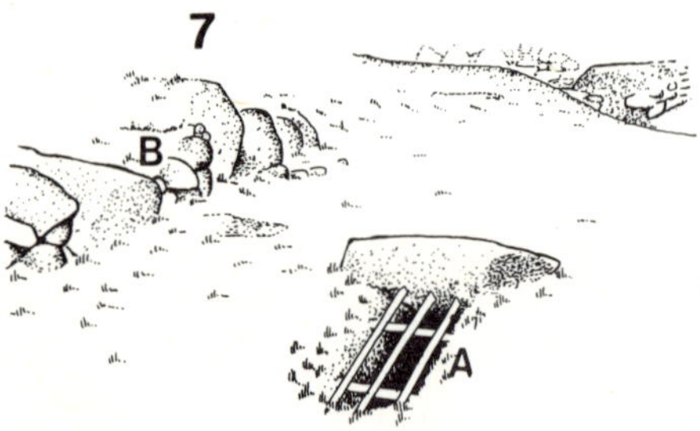


◀ **A** was probably the original entrance into the fogou. Wall **B** is later than the rest, being built differently and over the top of the others. It probably connected with the bend in the present field wall marked **Y** on the plan.

*The remains belong to four or five different periods – the underground chamber, the fogou passage and perhaps timber houses, the courtyard and round, stone built houses – ranging in date from at least the second century BC into the Roman period. The two basic building types were the simple hut and the courtyard house. The absence from the latter of round rooms comparable to those of Chysauster suggests that the courtyard houses here were either not domestic or wholly roofed. Padstones for posts were found only in the simple huts.*

Part of the present field wall, eg at **A**, incorporates remains of and is perhaps contemporary with the settlement. Between it and **B** there seems to have been a lane.
▼

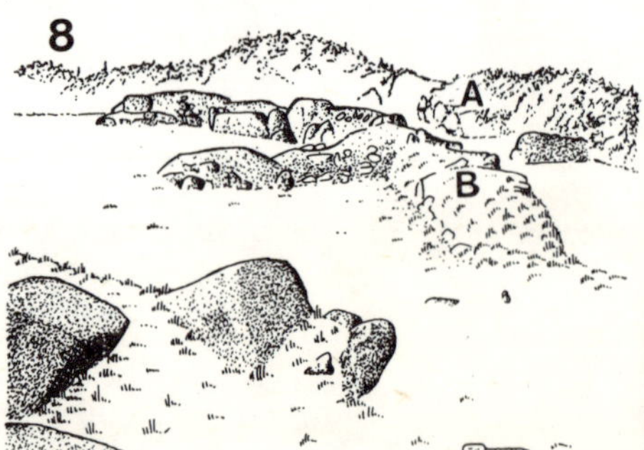

**3 Chun Castle and Quoit**
SW 404339

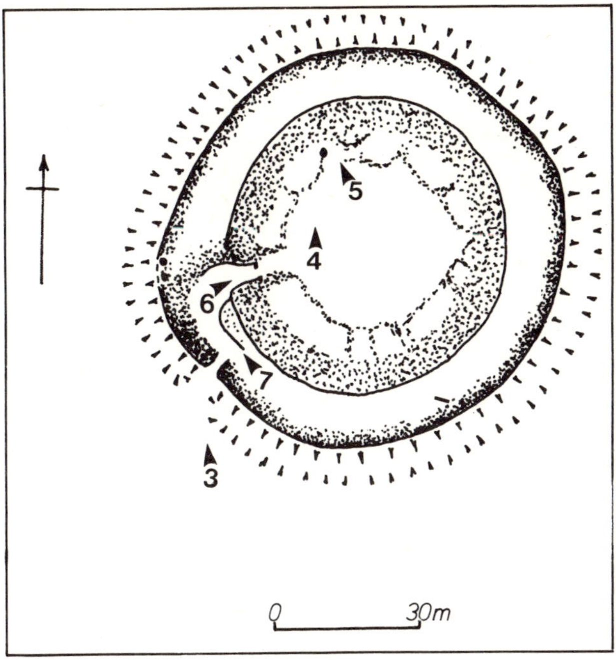


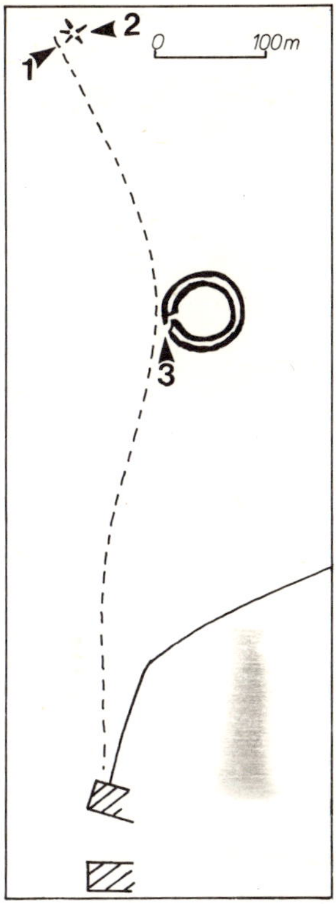


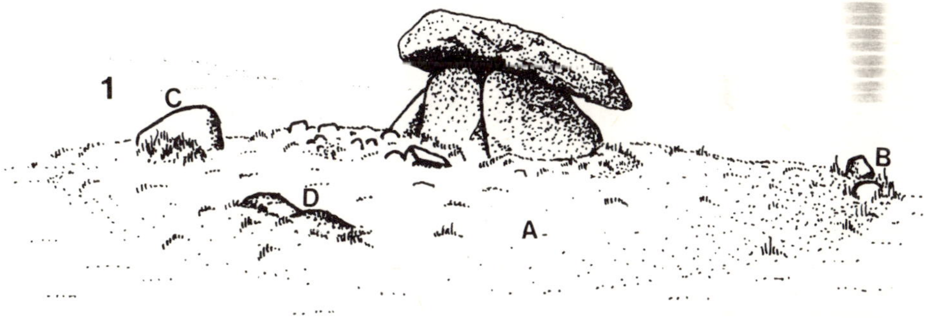


▲
The chamber stands within a mound **A** around the base of which was a kerb **B**. Stone **C** may have been part of that kerb but its axis is at right angles to the circumference of the mound. Together with prostrate stone **D** it probably formed an entrance, real or false. The latter is more likely as there is no evidence for a forecourt or passage between the two stones and the chamber.

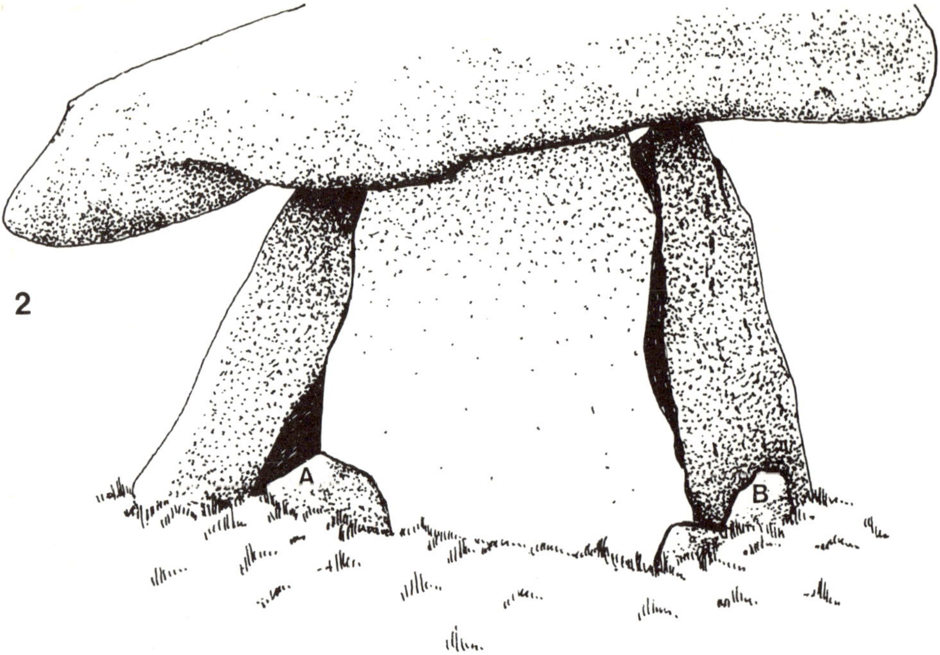


2

▲
The gaps between the slabs were closed by smaller stones such as **A** and **B**, and it is almost certain the sides always leant inwards. The excavator of 1871 found, however, little in the chamber. This he attributed to earlier robbing but it may be that there never were many burials within it.

*The megalithic chamber was enclosed by a mound around the base of which was a kerb. There is no evidence for a large number of burials within the chamber, but an entrance of sorts probably served as a focus for ritual and/or offerings.*

3

▲
The 'hillfort' has two ramparts with a ditch **A** in front of the outer one. The most remarkable feature is the quality of walling used in the ramparts. Originally they must have been higher and Borlase (1754) judged the ruins to indicate a former height of not less than 10ft for the outer rampart and 15ft for the inner one.

4

▲
The yards or buildings **A** against the back of the inner rampart **B** were found to overlie a number of circular huts. Such an arrangement of huts behind the wall is characteristic of the settlements called *Rounds*, eg the now destroyed site at Trethurgy:
Unlike Chun, however, *Rounds* usually have a single wall and date from the second century BC to the first century AD. Here the earliest material is third or second century BC.

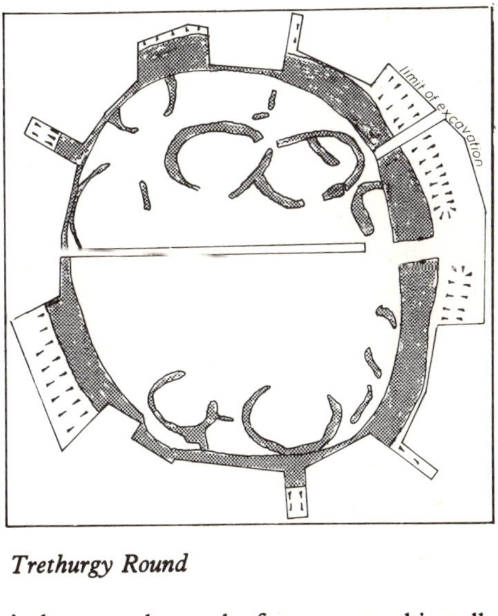


*Trethurgy Round*

5

At least one hut and a furnace near this well were in use in the sixth century AD. The metal smelting and contemporary pottery suggests the post-Roman occupants had some wealth and social standing, so it is reasonable to expect the defences to have been refurbished by them. It is also interesting to note the royal memorial of Men Scryfa is no further from here than the
◀ Tristan Stone from Castle Dore.

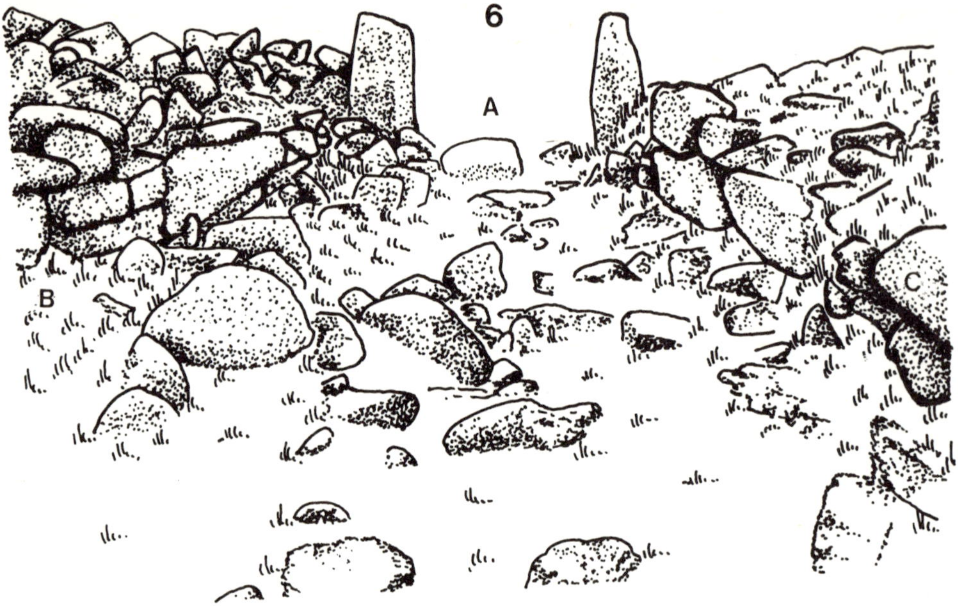


▲ The inner entrance was closed by gates at the end of the passageway **A** and a timber bridge may have linked the two flanking wall ends. Oddly one corner **B** is rounded while the other **C** is square, as if the passageway was originally approached from the left and not the right as now.

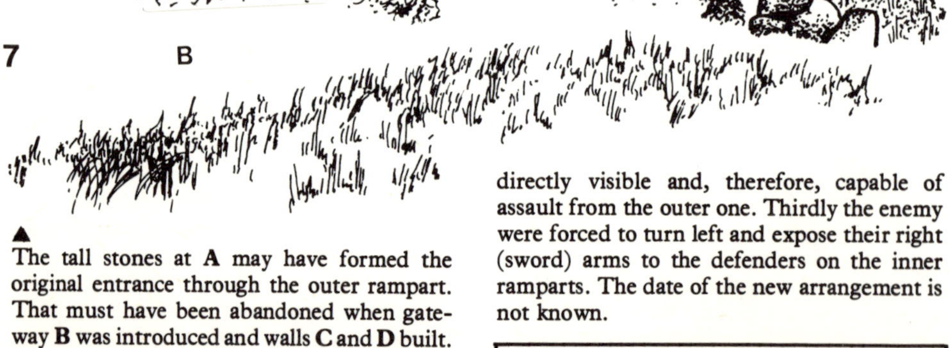


▲ The tall stones at **A** may have formed the original entrance through the outer rampart. That must have been abandoned when gateway **B** was introduced and walls **C** and **D** built. The new arrangements were militarily stronger than the old ones. Firstly **C** and **D** prevented the enemy who had penetrated the outer gate from seizing the area between the two ramparts. Secondly, the inner gate was no longer directly visible and, therefore, capable of assault from the outer one. Thirdly the enemy were forced to turn left and expose their right (sword) arms to the defenders on the inner ramparts. The date of the new arrangement is not known.

*The site shares certain features in common with* Rounds *and was occupied in both prehistoric and post-Roman times. The occupants were of high social standing.*

## 4 Men an Tol and Men Scryfa

SW426349 and SW427353

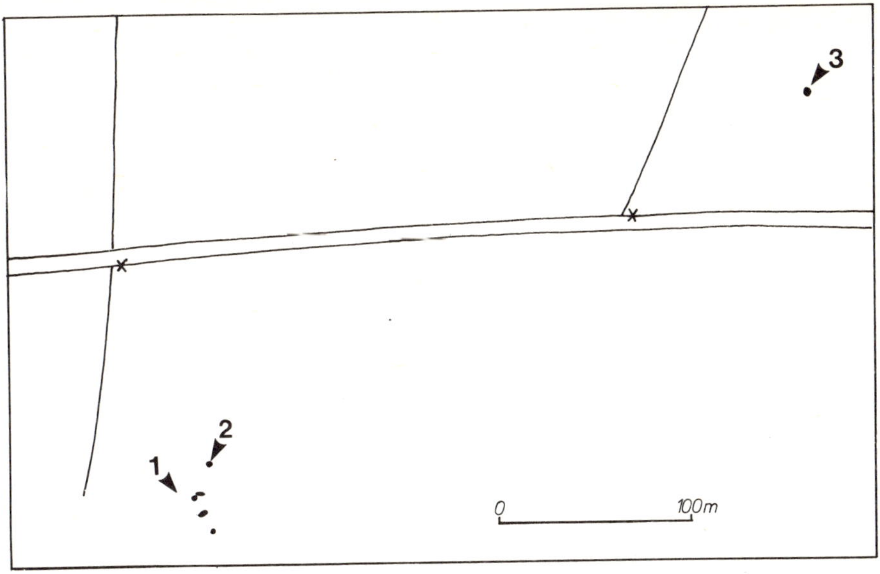

▲ Men an Tol has been claimed to be a prehistoric megalithic tomb with a 'porthole' entrance **A**, but there is no evidence for a chamber having existed either side of **A** and the latter is almost exactly halfway between stones **B** and **C**. While at least one stone is said to have been moved since 1815 the present appearance of the site may be much as the original builders intended. This is suggested by the presence of mound **D** for it is not unusual for paired stones to be associated with low mounds (see, for example, Merrivale **13**). Such arrangements indicate a relationship with those paired stones, posts or pits found in some Neolithic burial mounds. As some of those structures are considered to be also related to megalithic tombs it is perhaps not surprising this site has been described as such. The hole was formed by chipping or grinding from either side and until quite recently it was believed sick people and children with rickets could be cured if passed through the hole.

2

▲

The relationship of stone **A** to the others is not known.

*The original character of the site cannot be determined without excavation, but it was probably not a megalithic tomb. It may, however have shared a common ancestry with such structures.*

3

▶

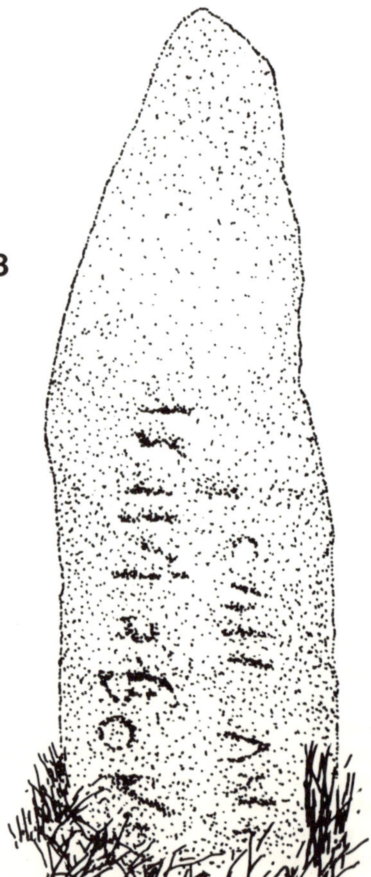

Men Scryfa — 'the stone of writing' — was felled in the nineteenth century by someone digging for gold. The inscription reads RIALOBRANI CUNOVALI FILI. *Cunouallos* comes from the British for 'famous leader' while *Ryalvran* seems to be Cornish, meaning royal raven. The inscription would thus read: 'royal raven son of famous leader'. In Celtic tradition the raven symbolised many things, not least war and death, and in local tradition this stone was erected after the death in battle here of Ryalvran. Legend places his centre at Lescudjack Castle (SW 475310) although Chun Castle with its post-Roman occupation is nearer.

*In the sixth century the area was ruled by a number of minor kings who did not always live peacably together. Their poetic tradition was Celtic and variants of many of the stories later recorded only in Wales and Ireland must have been told around Cornish hearths.*

## 5 Lanyon Quoit
SW 430337

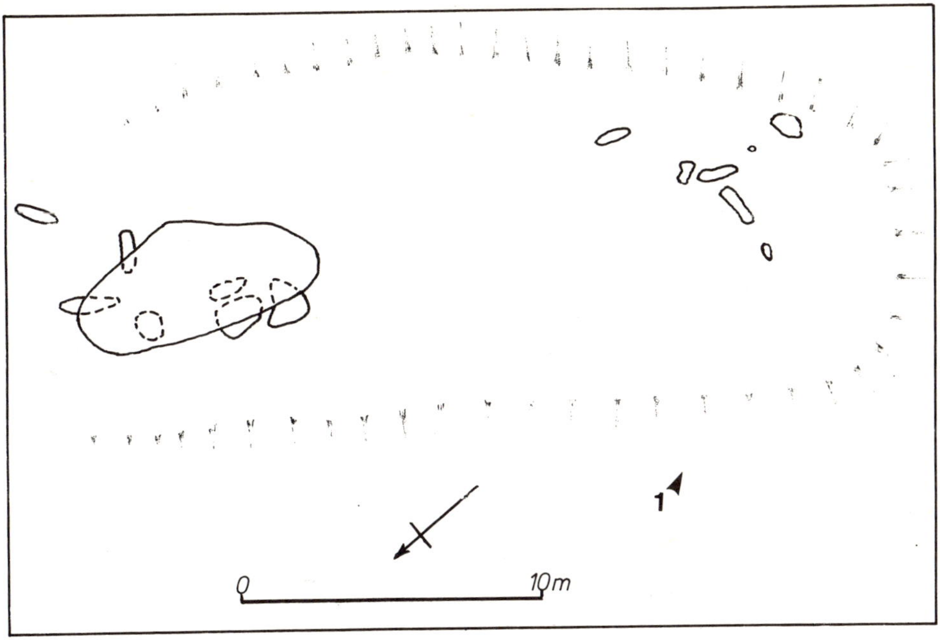


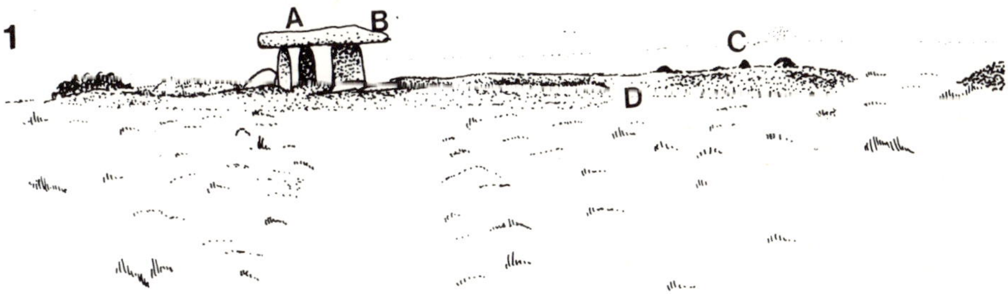


▲
The present appearance of the stones at **A** dates from 1824 when they were re-erected, for in 1815 the capstone **B** slipped, uprooting one vertical slab and breaking another. The existence of some stones at right angles to others suggests that the chamber covered by **B** had either a 'facade' or antechamber as at Zennor. A second quite separate chamber seems to be represented by the stones at **C**, the two structures being contained within a long rectangular mound **D**, which by analogy implies a Neolithic date. Excavations of other comparable sites has shown that separate chambers often had their own small mounds until finally joined. Why they should be remodelled is not readily apparent, but long mounds obviously belong to a different building tradition than round ones.

*The site consisted of one, possibly two, burial chambers within a long mound. A Neolithic date is implied.*

**6 St Buryan: Tregiffian, the Merry Maidens and Pipers**
SW433245

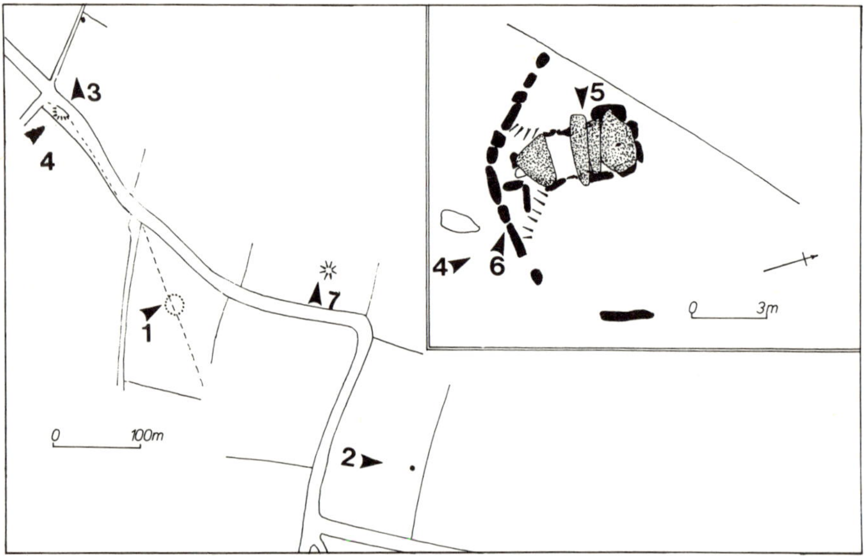

▲

The name of this circle, Dans Maen — Stone Dance — or the Merry Maidens reflects the tradition that the stones were humans petrified for profaning the sabbath. Although three members are known to have been replaced, the rough levelling of the tops of the stones, eg at **A**, is probably an original feature as is the gap between the stones at **B**. The pair of stones **C** and **D** recall those at the Hurlers **3** and may be unrelated to the circle. They are unlikely to have formed an astronomical alignment for a line at right angles to their axis does not pass through the centre of the circle. Their proximity to the circle does, however, echo the timber 'facades' of some timber circles such as Croft Moraig in Scotland, where the site was replaced by a stone ring. ▶

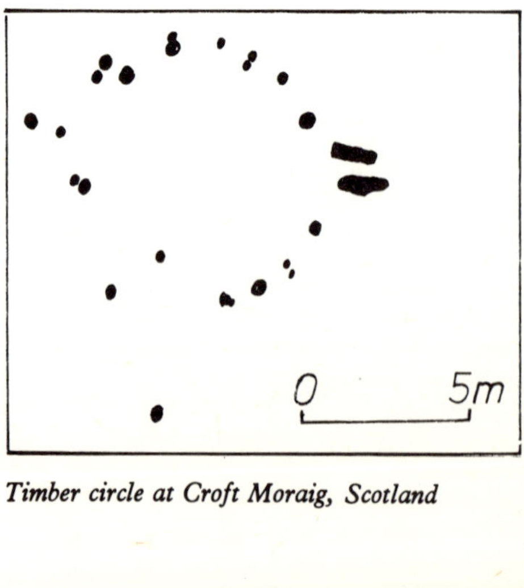


*Timber circle at Croft Moraig, Scotland*

2

3

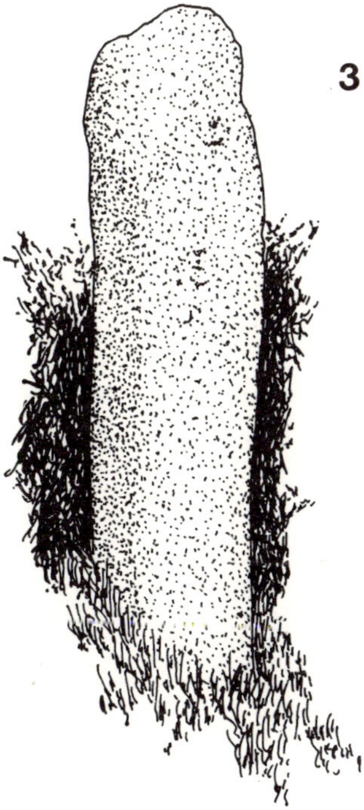

▲ Tradition identifies these two stones with the Pipers who played to the Merry Maidens, but they can hardly be said to be paired like those at the Hurlers. Rather they recall the individual monoliths at sites like Rudston in Yorkshire. There a late Neolithic-Early Bronze Age date can be ascribed to the stones. Here excavation at the foot of **A** failed to find anything.

◀ Similarly, excavation around this stone in 1872 found nothing. More recent excavation of a now destroyed standing stone near St Austell showed, however, that there the stone had replaced an earlier one which had replaced a pit and that in turn a timber post. The latter serves to remind us that timber posts may have been as common as monoliths. Some timbers were as heavy as the surviving standing stones and the engineering techniques used for the latter were probably developed on those earlier, less durable examples.

**Tregiffian**. The chamber at **A** was encased in a mound of turf with a perimeter of stones. Later the mound was reduced in size and the kerb **B** remodelled to a polygonal plan. ▼

4

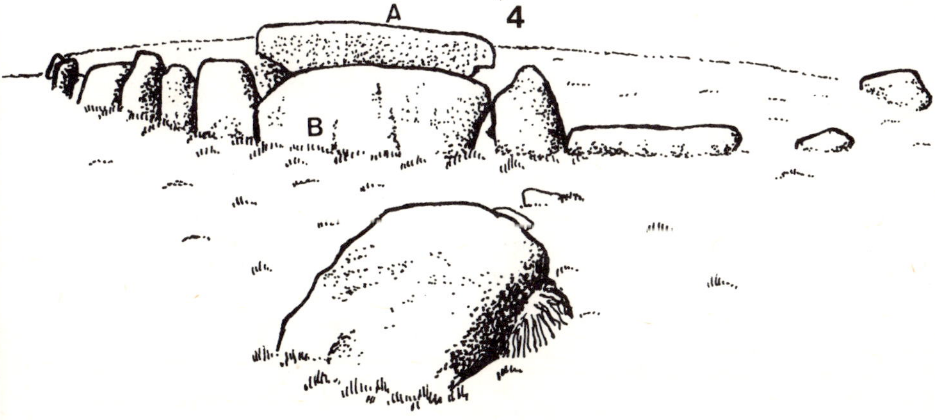

Capstone **A** contains a 'cupmark' or artificial ▶ hollow **B** on its upper surface with a similar carving underneath.

**5**

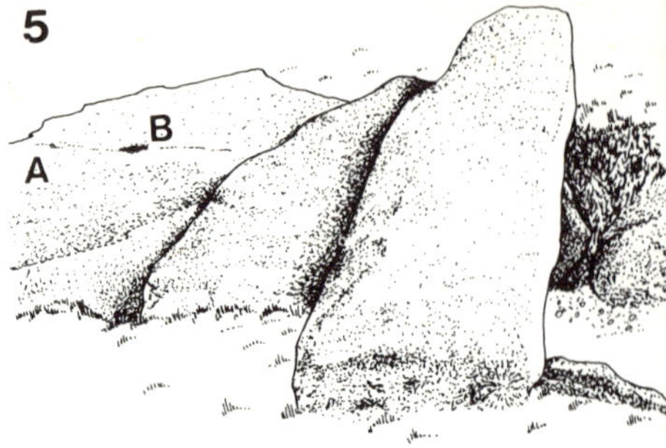


Far more elaborately decorated is stone **A** — a copy, for the original is now in Truro museum. By analogy such carvings are late Neolithic-Early Bronze Age in date and significantly Bronze Age pottery was found in two pits in the floor of the chamber while Neolithic pottery was in the old soil buried beneath the mound. It is tempting to date the polygonal kerb to the Bronze Age and the earlier structure to the Neolithic. It may simply be, however, that the tomb was built in an area of Stone Age occupation. The pits recall that of Zennor but the chamber there is built in a different tradition to this one. There the structure is a tall box, here it is a low rectangle or gallery, but at both sites the chamber seems to have been sealed in the Bronze Age.

▼
**6**

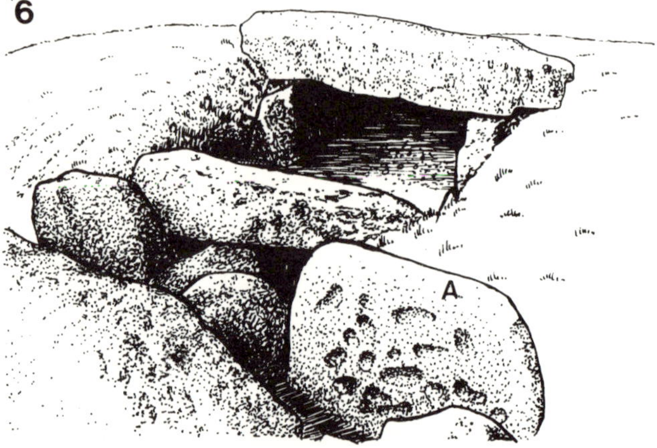


**7**

▲
Desultory excavation of this mutilated round mound produced an urn, probably Bronze Age in date. Another was found in a now destroyed mound at SW433246, while a cist containing a 'Beaker' was ploughed up at SW431243.

*The area was of considerable importance in late Neolithic-Early Bronze Age times and some of the ritual structures may have been erected in areas of earlier occupation. The megalithic tomb remained in use into the Bronze Age while the stone circle and standing stones link with timber structures.*

**7 ZENNOR QUOIT**
SW 469380

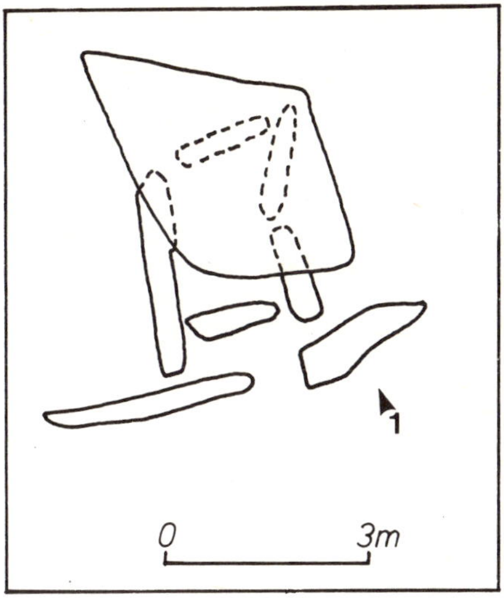


The front stone of the main chamber is set back a little to make an antechamber **A** beneath the floor of which were found a Bronze Age pot and whetstone. While stones **B** and **C** help form the antechamber they also provide a 'facade'. Such a 'facade' was probably intended to be seen, with the stones visible much as they are now, while the chamber was in use. The construction of a mound over all the stones — if it ever occurred — would be the final act, and evidence elsewhere suggests it could occur hundreds of years after the chamber was erected. Here the Bronze Age objects probably represent a deposit made just before the raising of the mound. The only evidence for burial was a few cremated bones in the main chamber. Whether there was only ever a 'token' burial or whether the rest was robbed cannot now be determined. The chamber is known to have been damaged and an eighteenth century drawing shows the capstone **D** horizontal.

▼

*Whether the structure was used wholly for burial or other related purposes cannot now be determined but the antechamber probably remained accessible through its facade for some time. The final sealing of the chamber(s) took place in the Bronze Age.*

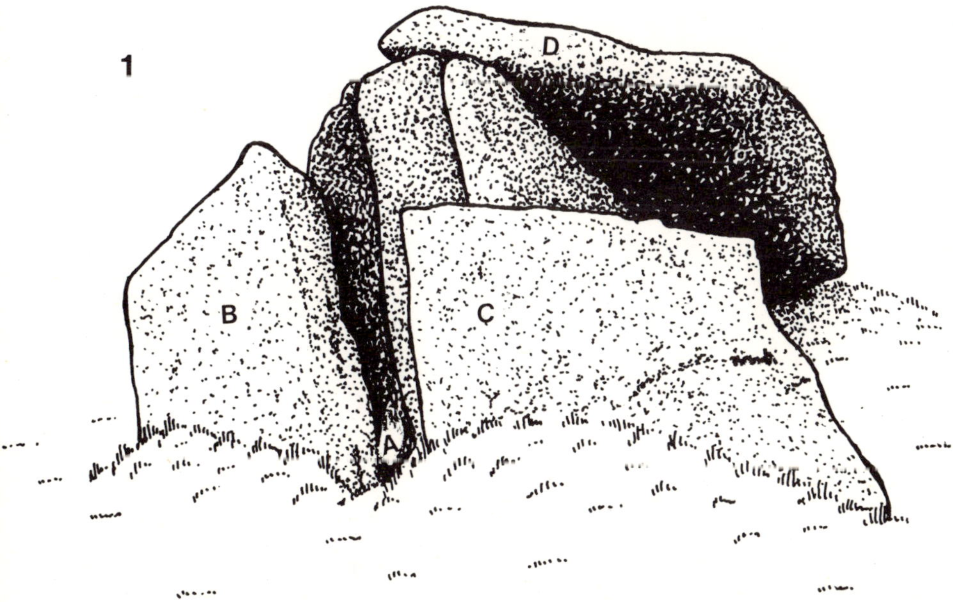

## 8 Chysauster
SW 473350

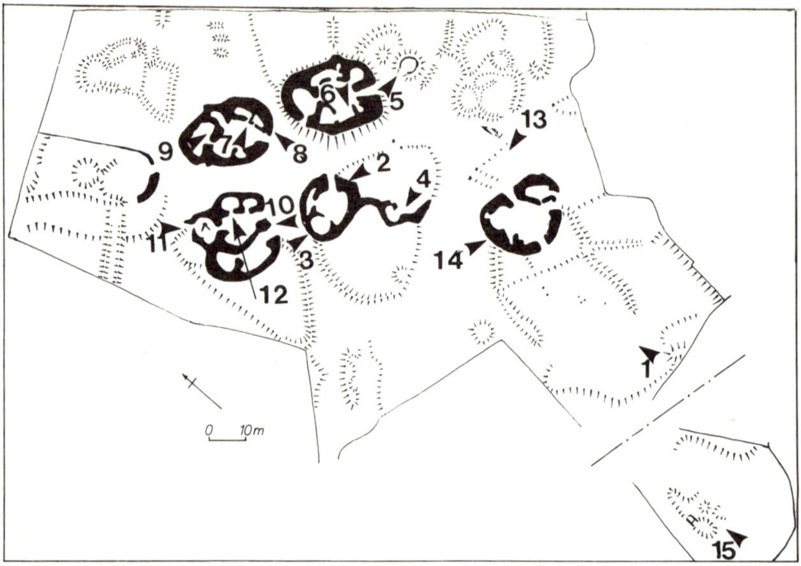

▲
The huts, eg **A**, are grouped together but have no enclosing wall or rampart. Adjacent to each is a plot of land **B**, between which are lanes like **C**. The lanes must have led through the fields to open grazing land. Not all the buildings have been excavated but the material recovered suggests occupation from the second century BC to the second century AD.

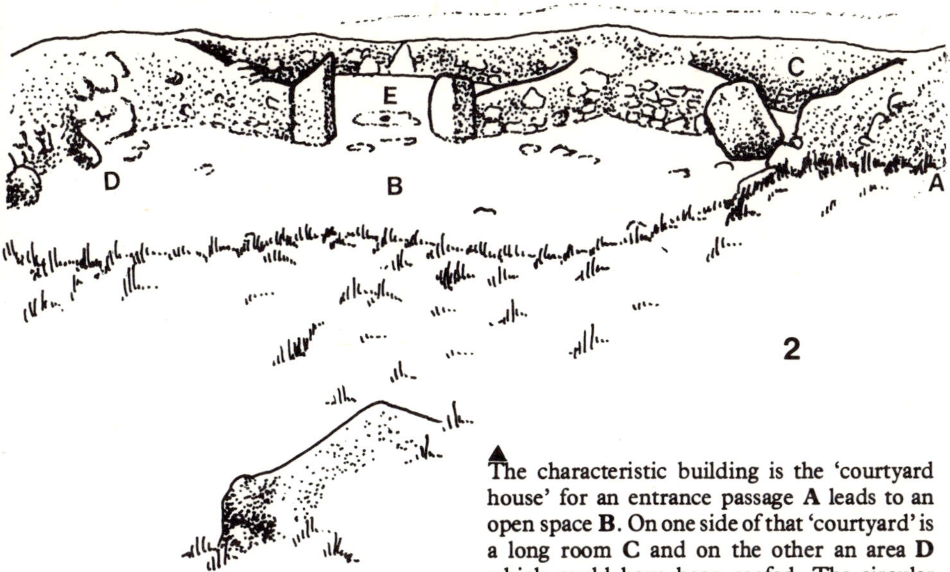


2

▲ The characteristic building is the 'courtyard house' for an entrance passage **A** leads to an open space **B**. On one side of that 'courtyard' is a long room **C** and on the other an area **D** which could have been roofed. The circular area such as **E** usually contained most finds and seems to have been for domestic use. **D** may have been a byre.

3

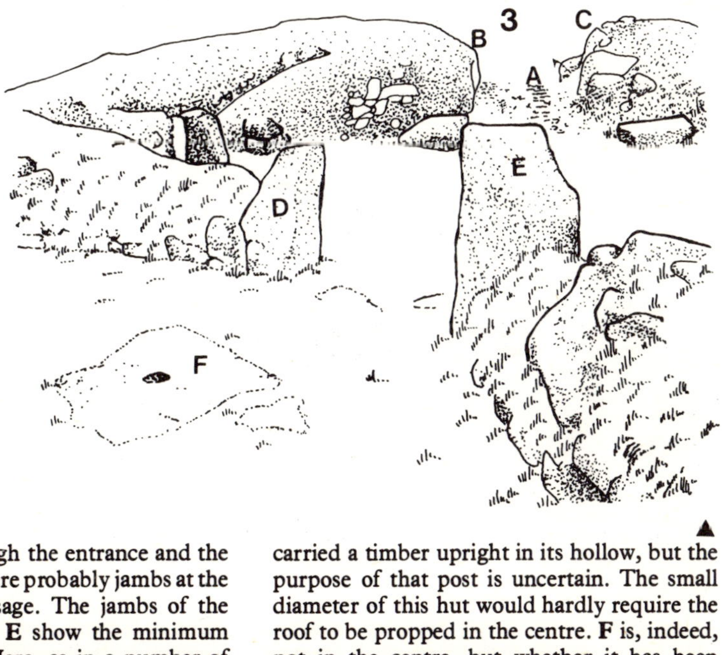


▲ A drain **A** runs through the entrance and the two stones **B** and **C** were probably jambs at the inner end of the passage. The jambs of the domestic area **D** and **E** show the minimum height of the walls. Here, as in a number of other huts, there is a padstone **F**. The padstone carried a timber upright in its hollow, but the purpose of that post is uncertain. The small diameter of this hut would hardly require the roof to be propped in the centre. **F** is, indeed, not in the centre, but whether it has been moved or not is unclear.

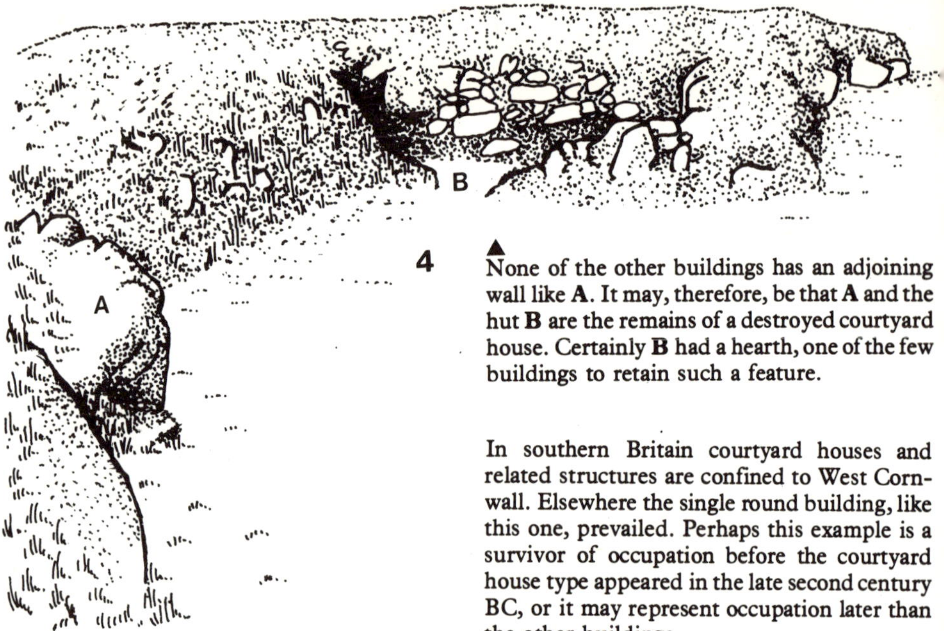


4

▲ None of the other buildings has an adjoining wall like **A**. It may, therefore, be that **A** and the hut **B** are the remains of a destroyed courtyard house. Certainly **B** had a hearth, one of the few buildings to retain such a feature.

In southern Britain courtyard houses and related structures are confined to West Cornwall. Elsewhere the single round building, like this one, prevailed. Perhaps this example is a survivor of occupation before the courtyard house type appeared in the late second century BC, or it may represent occupation later than the other buildings.
▼

5

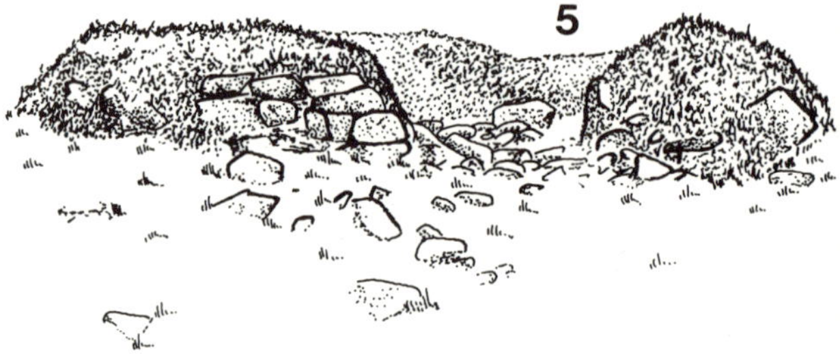

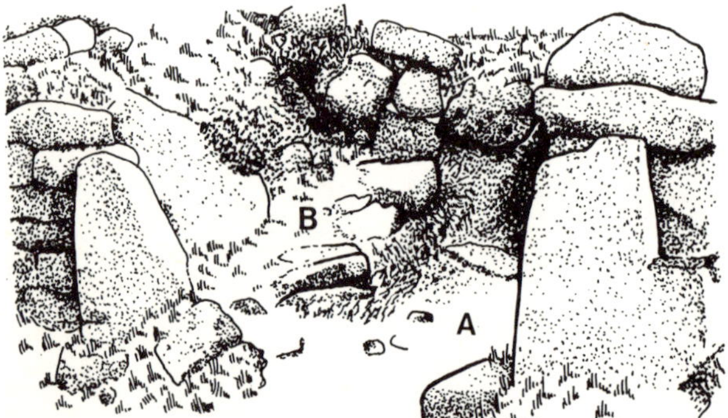


▲ 6

This recess is one of the few areas where the function is identifiable. A number of channels led into a sump at **A** and there was an overflow through the wall. **A** must have been to collect water and platform **B** to keep the feet of those using it dry.

7

▲
The raised, paved floor of **A** suggests that the room was used for storage and the corbelled niche **B** must have had a similar purpose. The builders may have intended to subdivide the long room **C**, for it was provided with two entrances **D** and **E**. A pit was found beneath the floor in the western half.

8

▲
This long room was certainly subdivided after its main wall **A** had been built.

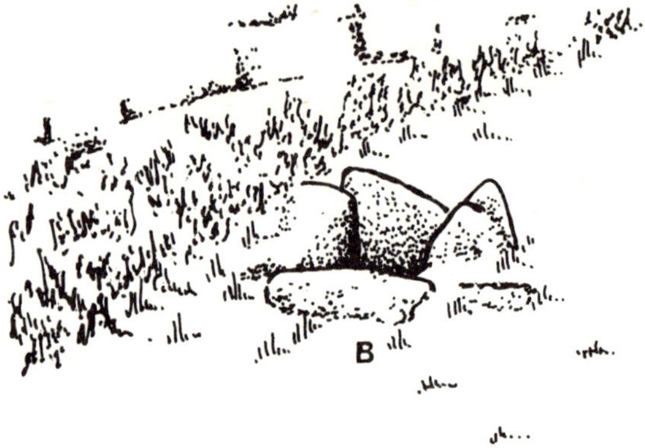


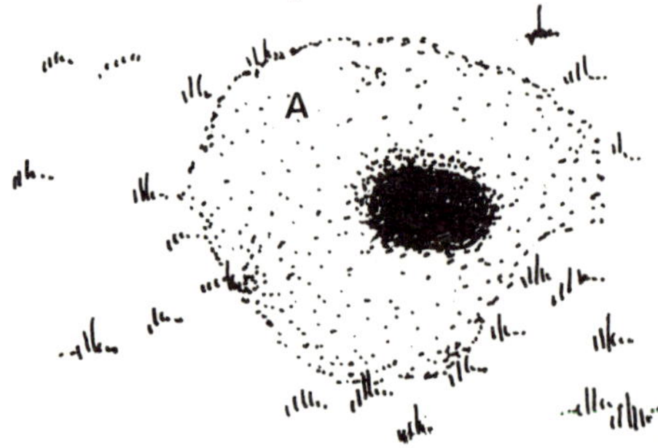


**9**

▲
Within this domestic area was the usual pad-stone **A** and the strange box **B** which must have held domestic or culinary items. There must have been many other containers in more perishable materials.

Here one complete courtyard house **A** has half of another alongside. The plan suggests that **A** has been built over an earlier house **B** but the excavator thought **B** had been added to **A**. Both seem to have been in use at the same time. The wall at **C** had to be rebuilt after excavation but an earlier collapse of the entrance may have occurred. The long stones **D** are said to have spanned the entrance passage, but the width of the latter makes the use of stone lintels improbable.
▼

**10**

▲
The round room has a back door **A** with a porch-like arrangement **B**. The purpose of structure **C** is unknown, but it was not a hearth for there was no evidence of burning. **C** may represent use of an abandoned building and is perhaps a pulpit, for in the early nineteenth century the site was occasionally used by Methodists and even known as the 'Chapels'.

▲
Instead of a single long room the builders here constructed two separate ones **A** and **B**, presumably because it was more convenient — compare **7C** and **8**. Whatever the reason, the idea of the long room being on the right of the entrance and the byre on the left remained. The padstone **C** is said not to be in its original position and it is usually considered that the courtyards were not roofed. The evidence is, however, inconclusive. It would certainly have been possible to roof the courtyards and it is difficult to see why the overall shape of the building was approximately round and the rooms so small if they were not under a single roof. Constructing separate conical roofs over **A** and **B** would have been very difficult particularly on wall **D**.

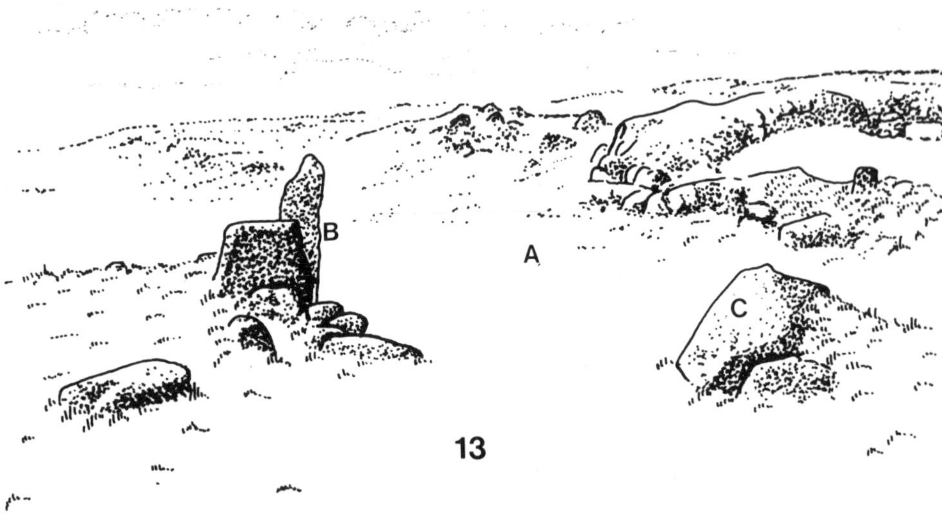


▲
The houses appear to be built along a lane **A** and from what seem to be gateposts **B** and **C** a slight hollow leads to the door of the adjacent building. The existence of gateposts implies that the sides of the lane were originally carried up to some height, perhaps by turf or stone and soil banks.

▲
The pottery from this house was later than elsewhere and the building seems to have been altered in antiquity. Door **A** was created when the original **B**, with its remaining jamb **C**, was blocked. Interestingly it is **A** which leads to the gateposts **13B** and **13C**.

15

The fogou is presumably related to the settlement.

*The buildings were primarily 'courtyard houses' in use from the second century BC to the second or third century AD. Not all were contemporary and some alterations occurred to individual structures. Each seems to have possessed its own croft and to have been built at the side of a lane. Evidence here and elsewhere indicates a well developed network of roads long before the Romans came.*

## 9 PHILLACK
SW565385

The Chi Rho monogram **A** is a fairly common Christian symbol in Roman Britain, occurring on lamps and pottery and, more rarely, in mosaic pictures. The symbol seems to have survived into the post-Roman period and a sixth-century date is suggested here. That it was carved on stone implies the existence of a Christian building, presumably a church. The former shape of the churchyard — circular — is also evidence for an early Christian centre.

1

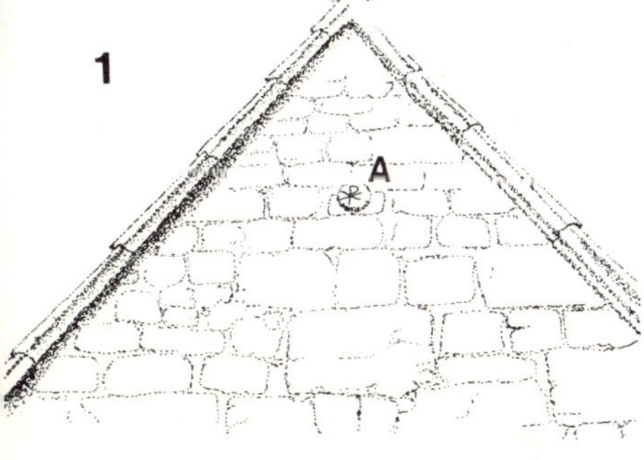


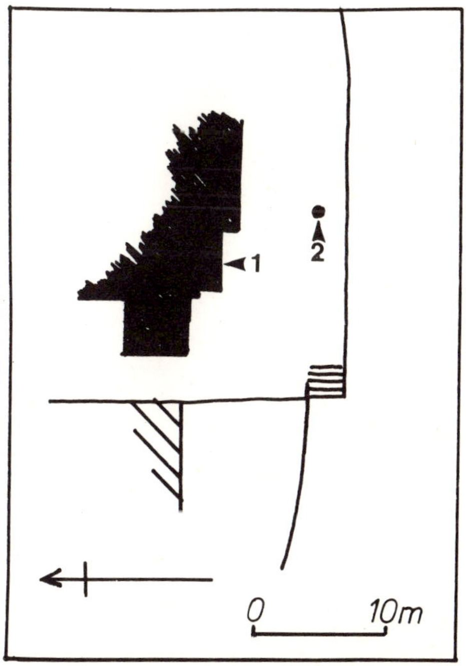

2

◀ Finds made when the churchyard at **A** was removed to widen the road included a piece of late Roman pottery, as well as a number of burials in cists. The latter are, however, thought to have been medieval in date. The date of the cross is somewhat uncertain. It has interlace ornament **B** similar to that on a number of crosses, such as Cardinham (SX123687). The decoration of the latter — also in a circular churchyard — has Irish-Norse parallels, suggesting a tenth-century date. The angular motif here **B** may be later but the figure of Christ **C** seems to have a vertical line on each wrist, a feature found on another carved, but very worn, stone from this site. The stone is considered by Prof. C. Thomas to be the front of an altar belonging to a time after the eight century.

*Cardinham Cross*

2a

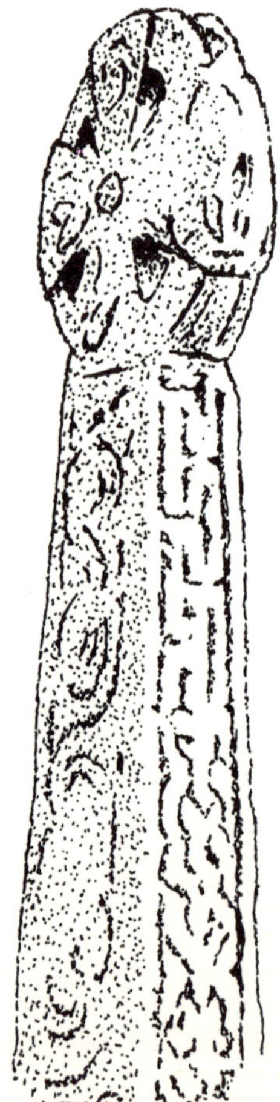

*Some still functioning churchyards seem to have been centres for Christian communities as early as the sixth century. They show how easily ritual and tradition can survive centuries of social and political change.*

## 10 Carn Brea
SW 686407

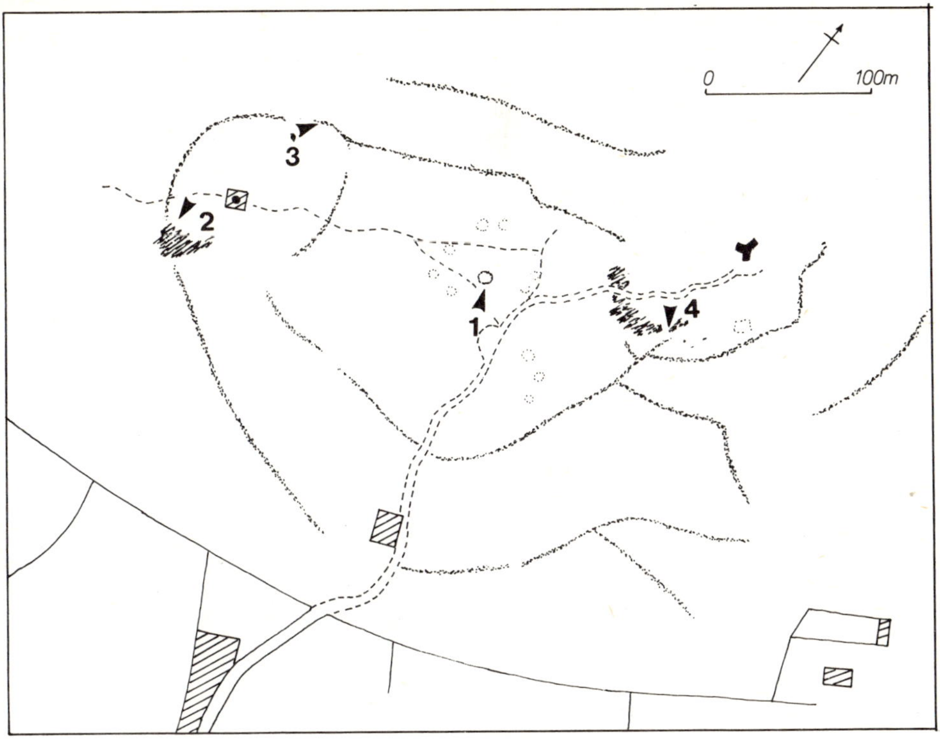

1

▲ The hill was inhabited long before the castle — only parts of which are medieval — was built. The most conspicuous remains of that early settlement are the hut circles. This one has been dated by excavation to the Early Iron Age and was found to be built over a soil tilled in Neolithic times. A number of Neolithic field clearance cairns have also been identified and cultivation may have been by hoe. The hut appears to be roughly contemporary with the bronze objects found in the eighteenth century and subsequently dated to 800-650 BC. Later prehistoric and Roman occupation is implied by the coins found hereabouts, and a small bronze mounting shaped like a bull's head also belongs to that period.

2

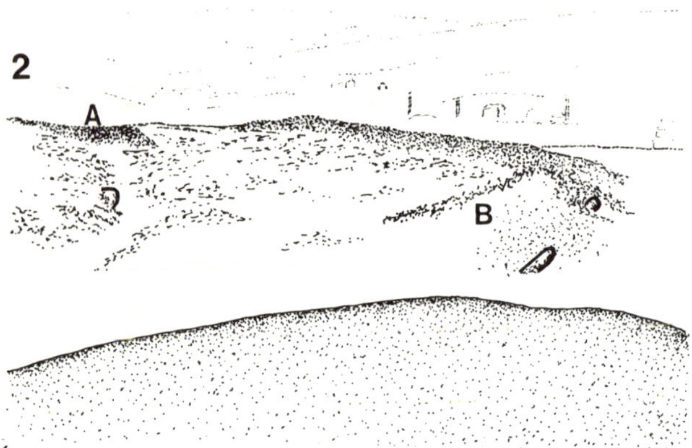


▲
Perhaps contemporary with the hut circle, perhaps later, the hilltop was enclosed by a number of ramparts like **A** and **B**. Such widely spaced ramparts make the 'hillfort' more like Milber Down than Hembury.

3

The ramparts seem to have been walls with slab faces **A** and rubble cores. A branch of this one enclosed the high ground around the monument forming an area once known as the Old Castle. ▶

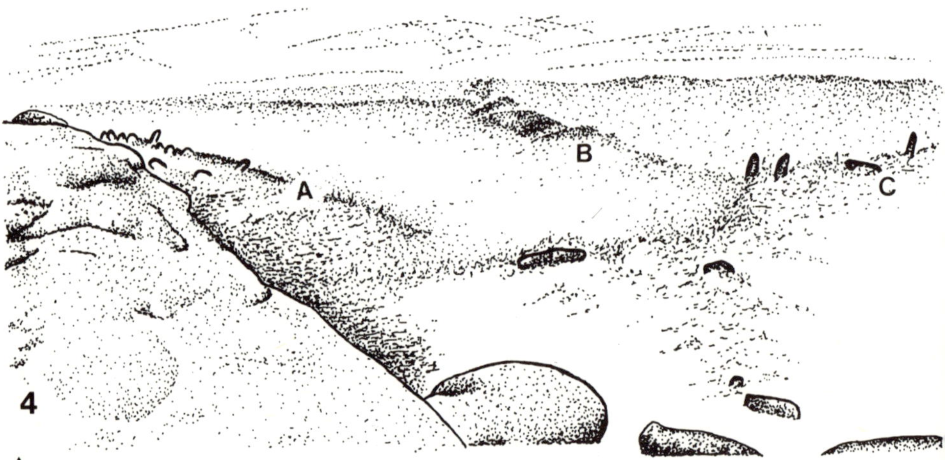


4

▲
However, not all the ramparts — eg **A, B** and **C** — are contemporary. **A** was built over fresh Neolithic material and must have formed a Stone Age hilltop enclosure. Inside and against that early rampart was at least one rectangular timber building, while beyond was the cultivation noted at **1**.

*Settlement on the hilltop can be attested at various periods, in the Neolithic, in the Iron Age and perhaps in Roman times.*

**11 Trevelgue**
SW 825630

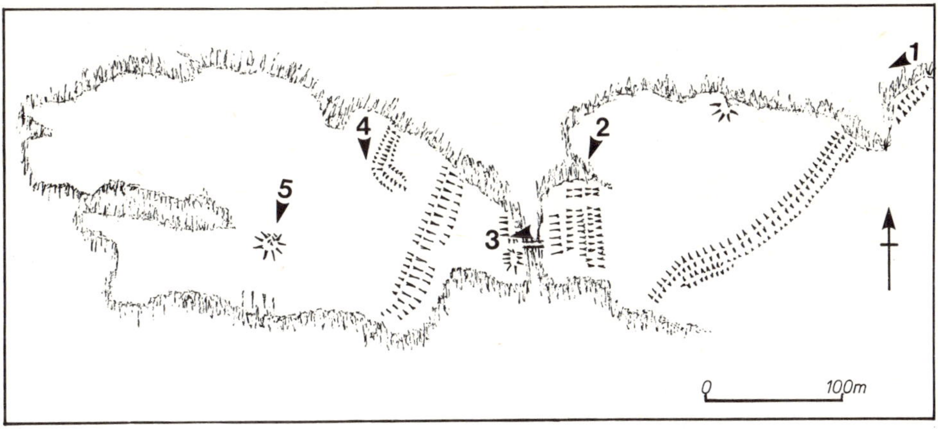


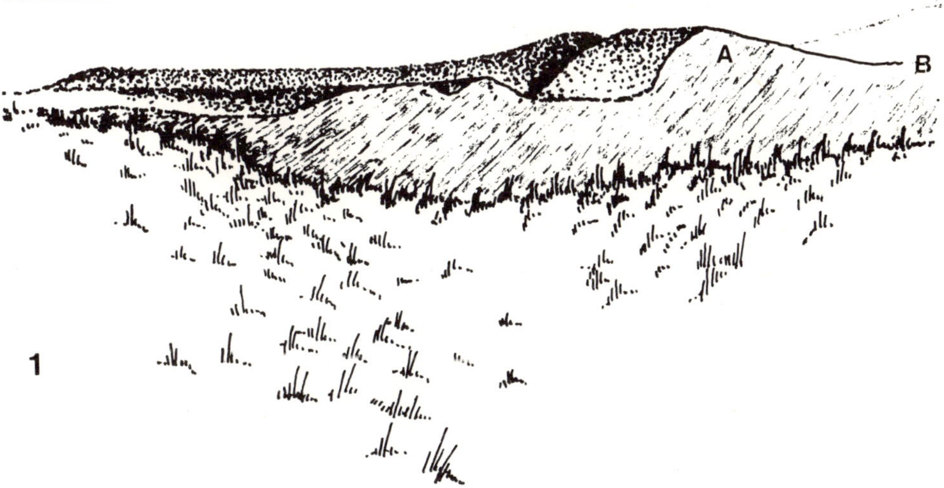


▲
The headland was fortified in the Iron Age by the construction of a series of ramparts such as **A** between the cliffs. This type of site is thus sometimes called a promontory fort. Burial mound **B** together with another (**5**) on the headland implies the area had been settled at least as early as the Early Bronze Age.

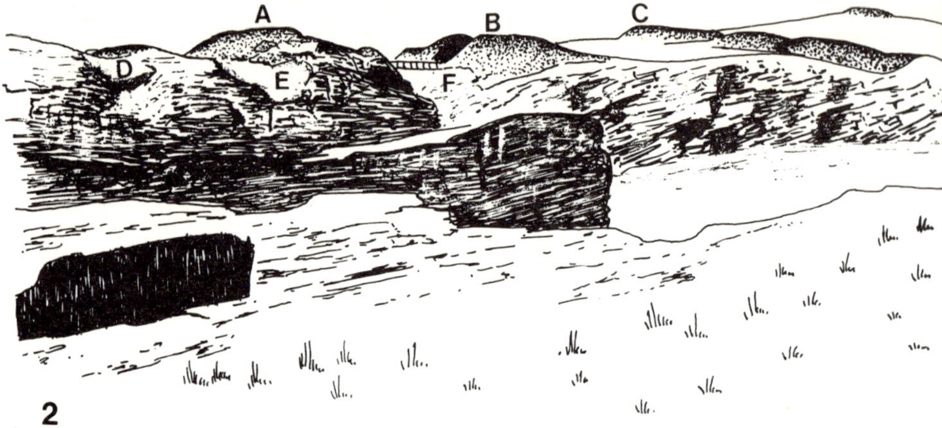


2

▲ The main Iron Age ramparts **A**, **B** and **C** were concentrated some distance from **1 A** where the neck was narrowest and where presumably there was still a land bridge. The size and shape of the two surviving ditches can be seen at **D** and **E**. The third ditch and rampart **C** is separated from the others just as **1 A** is. Sites with widely spaced ramparts, eg Milber Down, are usually considered as a separate type of monument from 'promontory forts', so it may be there were two periods or phases of occupation here. Excavations in 1939, only briefly reported, dated the defences to the third century BC.

The ramparts were built by tipping material, eg **A** and **B**, dug from the ditch over the old ground surface **C**. ▼

3

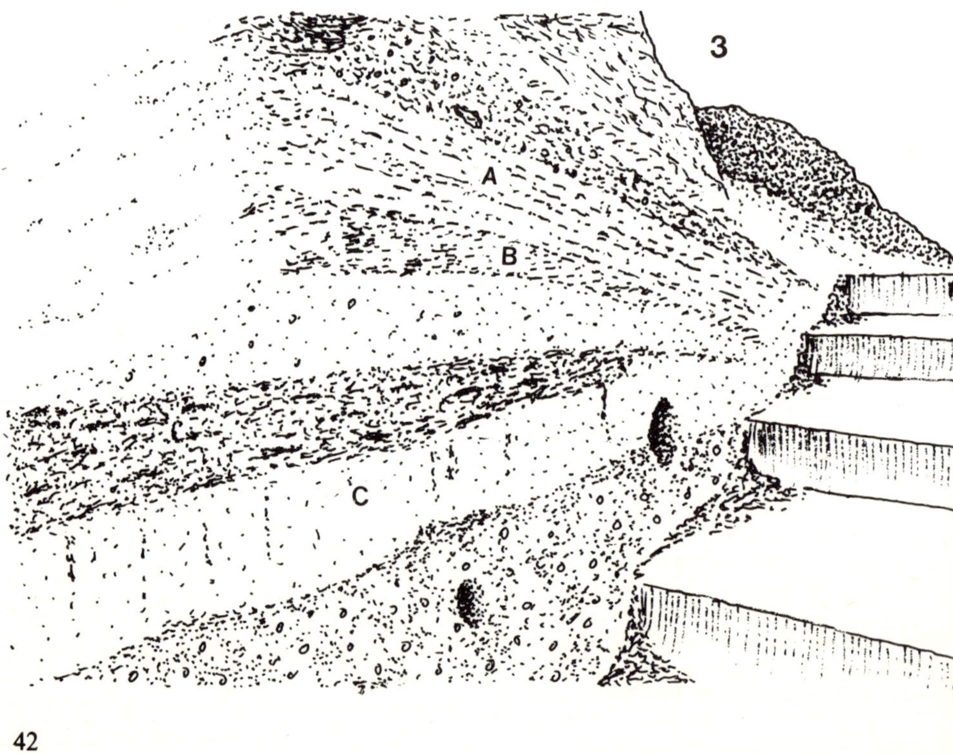

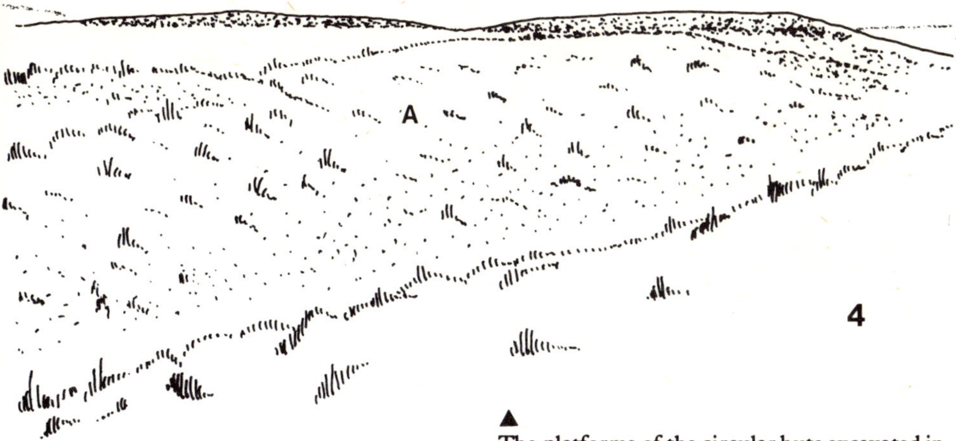


4

▲
The platforms of the circular huts excavated in the interior in 1939 cannot now be identified, but objects recovered dated from 200 BC to AD 120. During that period bronze and iron were smelted on the site. The rectangular earthwork **A** is reported to have been in use in the second and third centuries AD and represents a Romano-British farmstead. The excavator recorded one post-Roman structure.

5

▲
When dug in 1872 this mound was found to contain a cairn. There was no trace of a burial but **1B**, also dug at that time, had a burnt internment in a cup-shaped hollow. Scar **A** has developed from the excavation of 1872, for the method adopted was the sinking of a hole or trench in the middle of the mound, only expanding it if no 'goodies' were found. An examination of **A** reveals the lines of material slipped or pushed back into the excavation and some of the stones from the cairn.

*The headland was fortified in the third century BC and occupation continued at least until the third century AD. By that time the defences seem to have been abandoned and the isolated huts replaced by a nucleated or enclosed farmstead. Occupation continued into, or was re-established in, the post-Roman period.*

## 12 Pendennis Castle
SW824318

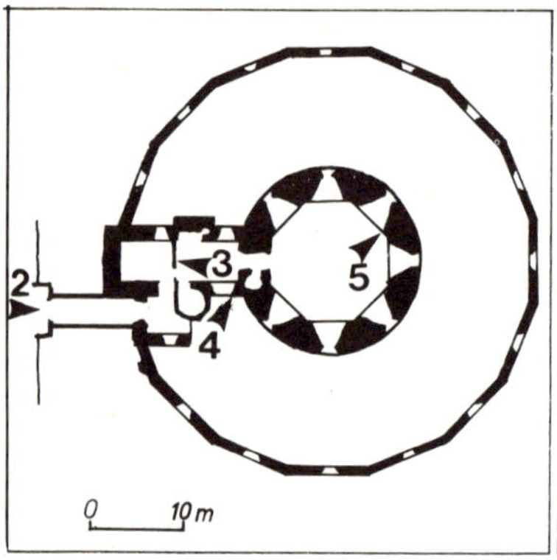


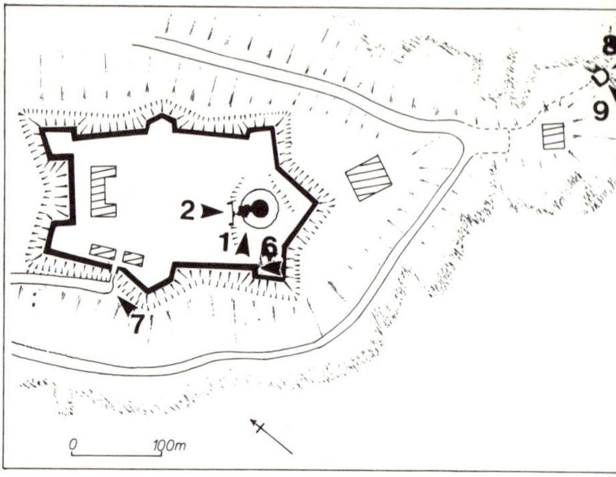


1

▲
The name, Pen *Dinas*, suggests there was a prehistoric hillfort in the area and a map of 1540 seems to show a rampart cutting off the headland. The map also shows that no work had been started on the surviving structure in 1540 while St Mawes was 'half made'. By 1546 both castles were finished. Henry VIII's castle consisted of a central tower **A**, curtain wall **B**, ditch **C** and, possibly, the governor's building **D**. There was a drawbridge across the moat and a guardhouse **E** at its outer end. The curtain **B** must, however, be a modification for it prevented guns firing from **F**. **D** is also an addition for a sixteenth-century plan shows a different entrance flanked by two towers. The guardhouse **E** may have been hexagonal like that surviving at St Mawes **1**. ▶

16th Century Plan

1a

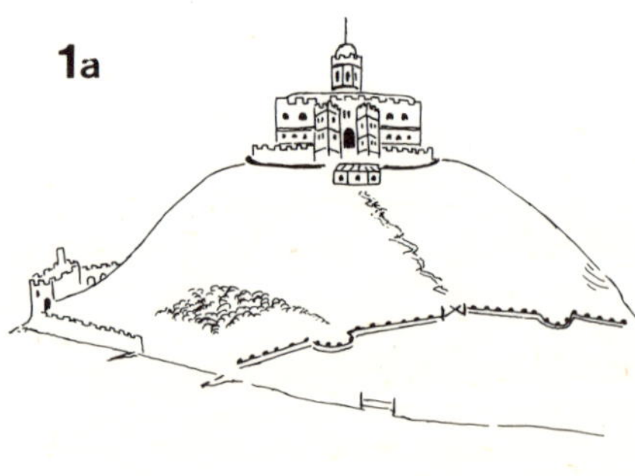

The coat of arms **A** indicates that the governor's building **1D** was added in Tudor times, possibly by Elizabeth I in 1598. Its entrance was protected by portcullis **B** and the drawbridge. The latter was replaced by **C** in the nineteenth century. ▶

Corbels **A** show that the present ceiling is somewhat lower than the original. To the left of the fireplace was a salt box **B**, while on the right was a small oven.
▼

◀ The jagged joints at **A** suggest that this doorway was altered or 'knocked through' when the governor's building was constructed. The door was secured by a drawbar **B** and anyone who succeeded in breaking through would come under fire from gunloop **C**.

The gunports were splayed inwards and outwards to allow a wide traverse for the cannons. The garrison was protected by 16 ft (5 m) thick walls but a vent, eg **A**, had to be provided above each gun to clear the smoke and fumes. ▼

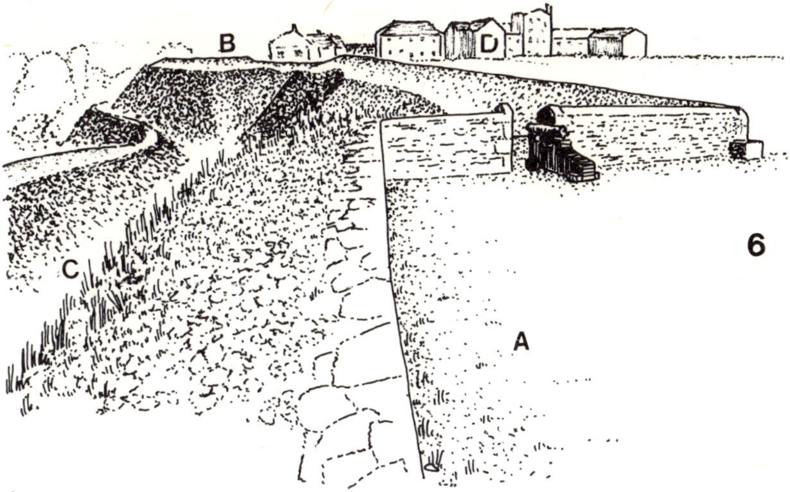


6

▲
In 1598 Elizabeth decided it was prudent to strengthen the site and a large fort was laid out. It was provided with projecting batteries, eg **A** and **B**, so the raking fire from the guns would cross. There was a rock cut ditch **C** and the ramparts were wide and battered to withstand or deflect enemy shot. So large and strong was the fort that during the Civil War it was held for the Crown by Colonel John Arundell and nine hundred others. Only famine caused them to surrender after five months and they were allowed to march out with honours. Then and in Elizabeth's time there must have been buildings within the fort. Those at **D** are relatively modern.

7

▲
The ornate entrance is said to have been finished in 1611, but shows no evidence for assault as one might expect after the siege of 1642, and a plan earlier than that portrays a simpler structure. The scale of the drawing may, however, have made the depiction of detail impossible, although the character of the drawbridge is clear. It was raised and lowered by counterweight, 8a.

8

▲ 'Little Dennis' is not shown on the map of 1540 so it must have been built later to complement the castle and, like that building, its battlements were battered **A** to reduce the impact of shot. Originally there were four guns at ground level, but they were reduced to three by the insertion of a larger portal **B** which effectively blocked **C** and **D**. On either side was a wall **F** and **G**. On the pre-1642 plan this wall is shown crenellated and enclosing an approximately rectangular area. A small ditch **H** protected its landward side and the entrance was covered by a bastion **I**. From there a path led up to the cliff top and a postern **J** in the main fort.

8a

*Plan earlier than 1642*

9 The roof top gun deck was supported by a heavy beam **A**. The roof was reached by a ◀ spiral staircase **B** and the door secured by drawbar **C**. There was also a fireplace **D** with oven **E** indicating that the men ate and slept amongst their guns.

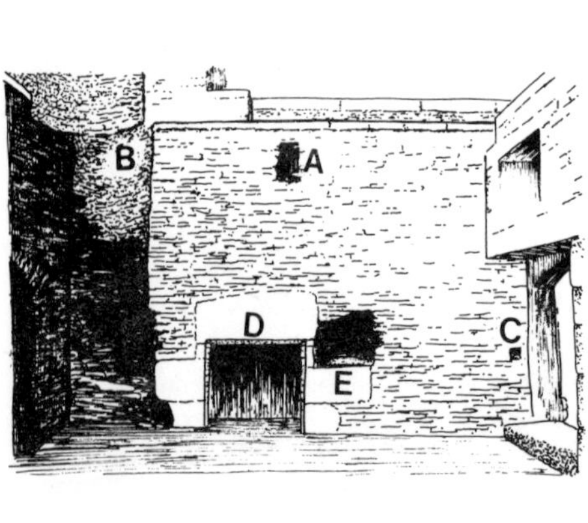


*Sometime between 1540 and 1546 Henry VIII fortified the headland with a castle, and in 1598 that was enclosed by a large star shaped fort. Both were designed for artillery and so effective were the defences the fort could not be taken by assault during the Civil War.*

## 13 St Mawes Castle
SW 841327

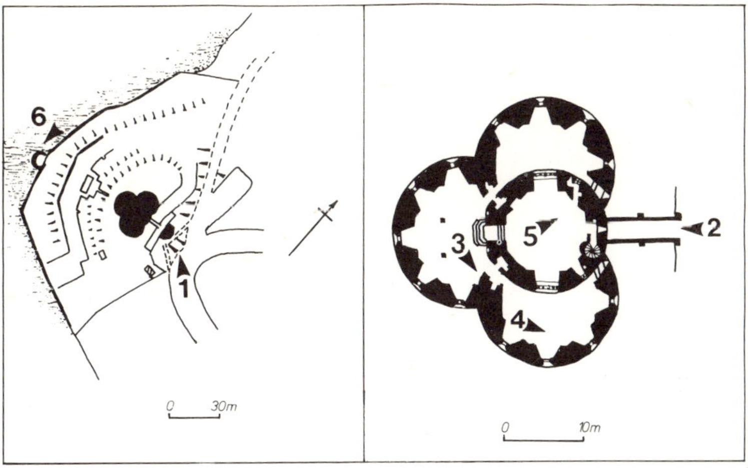

▲
The castle was separated from the hillside by a ditch and the only means of entry was by a bridge whose outer end was protected by guardhouse **A**. The hexagonal plan of **A** would have given the defenders 'all round fire' had they been on a flat site or hilltop like Pendennis. Instead they were overlooked by higher ground and, not surprisingly, the castle was surrendered during the Civil War without a fight. The castle was not designed to withstand major assault from the land (unlike the Elizabethan fort at Pendennis), but to defend the coast from seaborne attacks.

◀ The timbers **A** occupy the site of the drawbridge which would have been covered by fire from **B** and **C**, **D** and **E**. Slits **F** and **G** were for the drawbridge chains. The plan of the castle is that of a cloverleaf with a central tower **H** and three lunettes, eg **B** and **C**, around it. Its shape thus differs from Pendennis and it is more highly decorated. Each lunette for example has an inscription just below the moulded course **I**.

▲
Each portal was splayed inside and out to give as great a field of fire as possible and those on the lower floor were equipped with heavy shutters mounted in **A**. Vents **B** helped removed the smoke from the guns and there were garderobes **C**. Provision was made for the central tower to be defended separately, the doors to the lunettes, eg **D**, being secured by drawbars **E**.

4

▲
The gun portals of the lunettes also had shutters **A** and vents **B** and **C**. On the landward side, where it was impractical to have long-range guns, loops for muskets **D** were substituted.

5

▲
Quatrefoil openings like **A** allowed those on the gun floors or in this mess room to command the stairs, yet there was no provision for securing the doors from the inside as at **3E**. Instead the doors opened onto the stairs. Presumably the builders considered that the stairs made massive assault impossible. The mess room itself was served by the kitchen below. The ceiling was lowered in the nineteenth century so it now intersects panel **B** which must have been intended to carry some decoration.

▲
Below the main structure was a blockhouse. It was designed with cooking facilities **A** and must, therefore, have been roofed. Either side of the blockhouse was a walled terrace, parts of which may be incorporated in the present sea wall. While the terrace could have been used to mount more cannon it was primarily to prevent access to the castle from the beach. Like Pendennis the site was garrisoned during the Napoleonic wars, the latter part of the nineteenth century and again during the 1914-18 war. To those periods belong the complex between the castle and blockhouse as well as the ceiling of the mess room **5**.

*St Mawes was begun a little earlier than Pendennis and there are both similarities and differences. Built to defend the coast, the site could never be defended by a strong assault from the landward side.*

14 **Tintagel**
SX050890

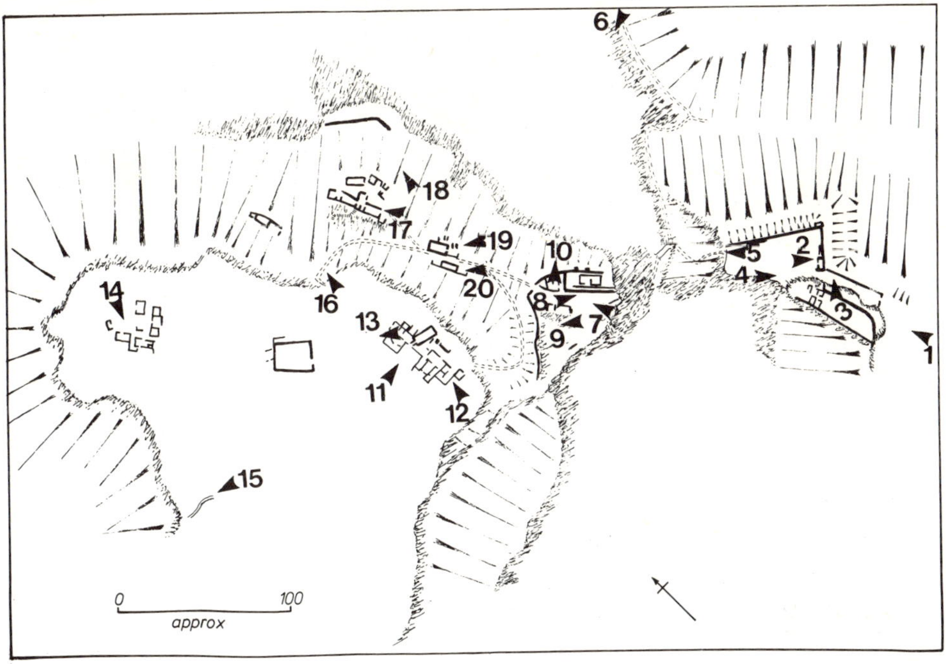


The landward half of the castle consisted of two wards **A** and **B**. The natural defences were augmented by the thirteenth-century curtain wall **C** and a ditch and rampart **D** which is thought to be earlier than the castle. The main gate **E** was reached along a revetted roadway **F**. This was defended by a gate at **G** which in the sixteenth century was said to have been 'guarded' with iron. **F** could not, however, be wholly covered by fire from the upper ward **A**.

▼

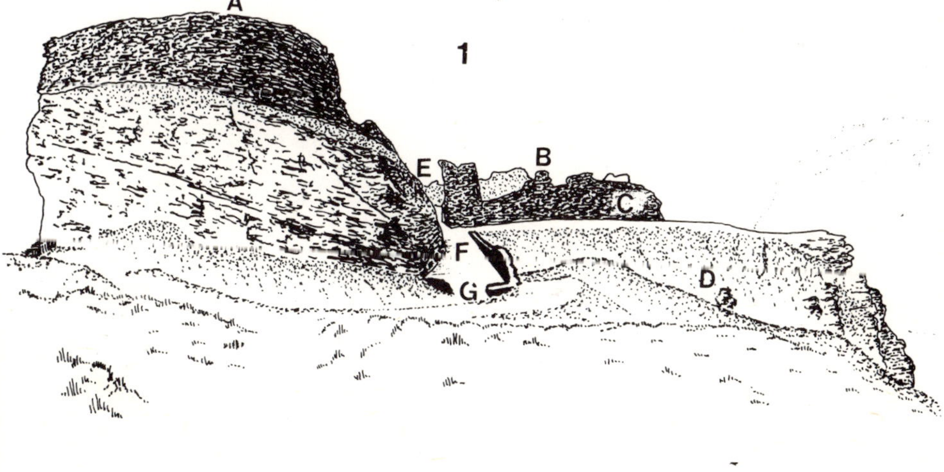

2

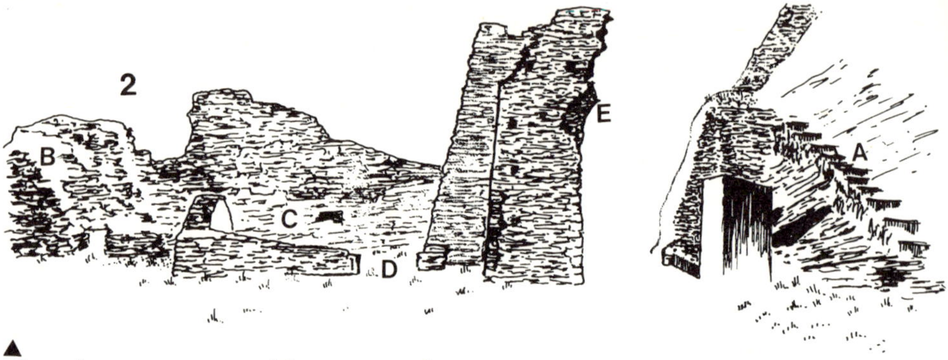


▲

The main gate was a tower with a room over the passageway. The room was reached from stairs **A** which also led to the upper ward. Ruined staircase **B** led to the parapet of the curtain, but was later abandoned when small building **C** was built across it. The doorway of **C, D,** has rebates for a wooden door frame and is thought to be late fourteenth or early fifteenth century. At that time the castle served as a state prison. The stones at **E** are the beginning of the arch over the main entrance.

3

▲

A few moulded stones, eg **A**, are the only other remains of that arch. Behind it were wooden doors secured by a drawbar **B**. The original passageway ended at **C**, extension **D** being part of building **2C**.

Approximately contemporary with **2C** are the wall **A** along the cliff edge of the upper ward and the buildings behind it. There must have been other structures, such as stables, in the lower ward.

▼

4

5

▲
The principal accommodation was on what is now the island. There wall **A** formed the eastern side of the twelfth-century great hall. Apart from the chapel no other twelfth-century structures can be identified. The early buildings must have been of timber and the defences, where not relying on nature, of earth and timber. Later a curtain wall **B** was added. Crenellation **C** and wall **D** are, however, nineteenth century. The castle thus seems to be no earlier than the twelfth century and probably replaced an earth and timber one at Bossiney (SS065888). In the twelfth century the island did not exist, there being a narrow neck of land which could be held by 'three men against the whole of Britain'. Two hundred years later it was necessary to construct a stone bridge where the neck had been. The bridge fell in the sixteenth century and erosion continues: the bottom of the concrete steps has had to be replaced by a timber bridge.
▼

5a

*Earthwork at Bossiney*

6

▲
In the fourteenth century the defences were augmented by the construction of a wall across the path from the small cove at **A**. The postern gate in the wall was closed by an iron door.

The western side **A** and northern end **B** of the early hall **5A** indicate that the building was 88ft (27m) long. Later it was narrowed and subdivided by walls **C** and **D**. Wall **E** formed the gable of a house built from the ruins of the second hall. At first it used wall **C** but that was later replaced by **F**.
▼

7

8

▲
The house had two rooms **A** and **B** and an upper storey reached by stairs **C**. It would seem that the cross wall **D** of the second period hall **7D** had two doorways **E** and **F**. **F** was later blocked while **E** had a timber door frame like building **2C**.

9

▲
This seems to have been a similar 'house'. There were two ground floor rooms, one with a fireplace **A**, and an upper floor reached by stairs **B**. Again there were wooden door frames.

▲
Wall **A** which blocked window **B** must also be contemporary for it too had door posts. There was a garderobe **C** and an upper floor **D**. The numerous holes **E** were for scaffolding, weathering having removed the material with which they were plugged.

▲
The castle's chapel **A** was entered through a porch **B** with benches**C**. **B** is an addition and replaces **D** which was walled up. The chapel has also been lengthened, the rough wall at **E** showing where the old eastern end stood. That the first chapel disregarded walls **F** and **G** show that the latter were ruined by the twelfth century.

12

▲

The buildings to which the clay bonded walls **11F** and **11G** belonged have been interpreted as a Celtic monastery. Rampart **1D** may have been a contemporary barrier, for it contained pottery like that in these buildings, and similar boundaries are known at other monastic sites. The pottery belongs to the late fifth or early sixth centuries and was imported, possibly with other goods such as wine, from the Mediterranean world. Masonry **A** is reminiscent of the tombs erected for the founders of other Celtic monasteries and, together with some rock cut graves on the opposite side of the castle chapel, suggests that the monastic church was hereabouts. The church would probably have been built better than the other structures and wall **B**, more massive than the others, may have been part. It is tempting to identify the site with Rosnant, the monastery where the relatives of Irish and other kings were sent for education.

13

▲

How long the site was occupied after the pottery ceased to be available is not known, but not all the buildings were contemporary. Wall **A**, for example, overlies **B** which is on an entirely different alignment. The castle garden **C** overlies a separate group of early buildings.

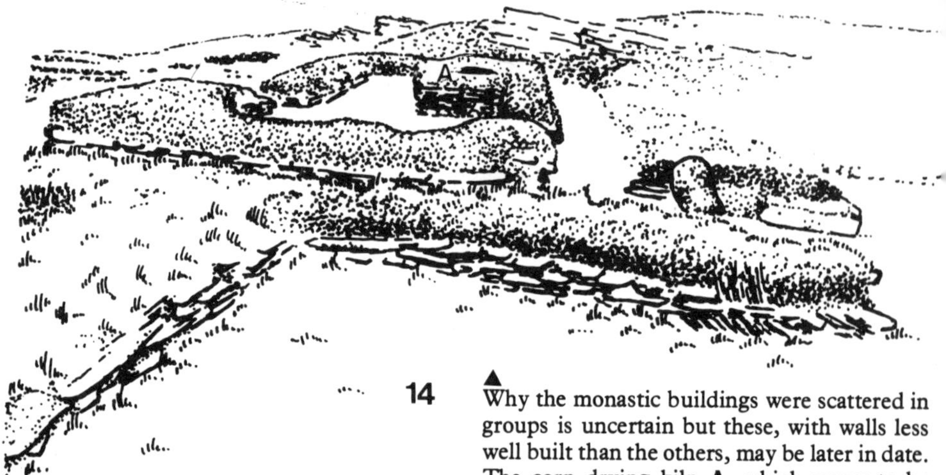

14

▲
Why the monastic buildings were scattered in groups is uncertain but these, with walls less well built than the others, may be later in date. The corn drying kiln **A**, which seems to be contemporary with the buildings, is almost identical to those at Hound Tor **4**. Either this type of kiln is as early as the monastery or, less likely, these particular buildings are thirteenth century. The kiln implies the growing of cereals, but where this occurred and on what scale is unknown. The existence of the castle garden suggests some soil was deep enough to support more than grass.

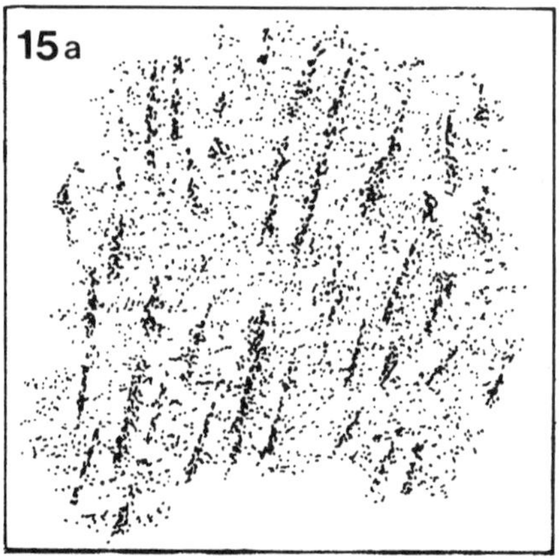

15a

◀ The tunnel is wholly or partly artificial for hundreds of short chisel marks can be seen on the walls:

The tunnel's purpose is unknown but it may relate to fogous like Carn Euny **4** and Chysauster **15**.
▼

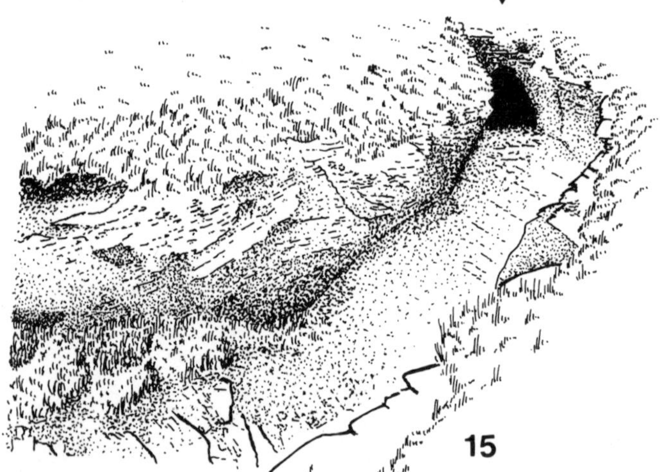

15

Given the large area of the headland, the creation of artificial platforms for buildings **A** must reflect the austerity the monks wished to practise. Spring **B** seems to have been utilised as a source of water.
▼

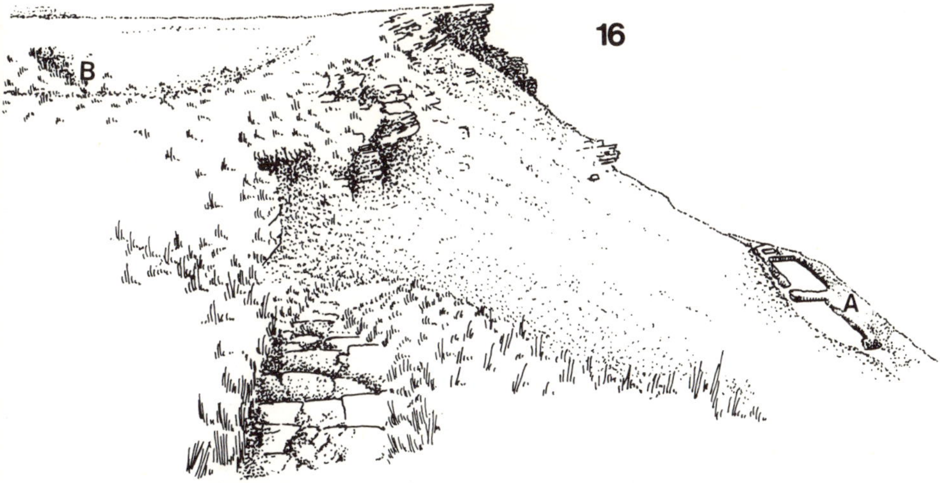


16

17

▲
The spring and the cliff top were reached, as today, by steps **A**. The long room **B** had an external bench **C** and probably served a communal purpose.

18

▲ Two of the small rooms have been interpreted as steam baths, because their floors were crazed as if by the sudden quenching of fires.

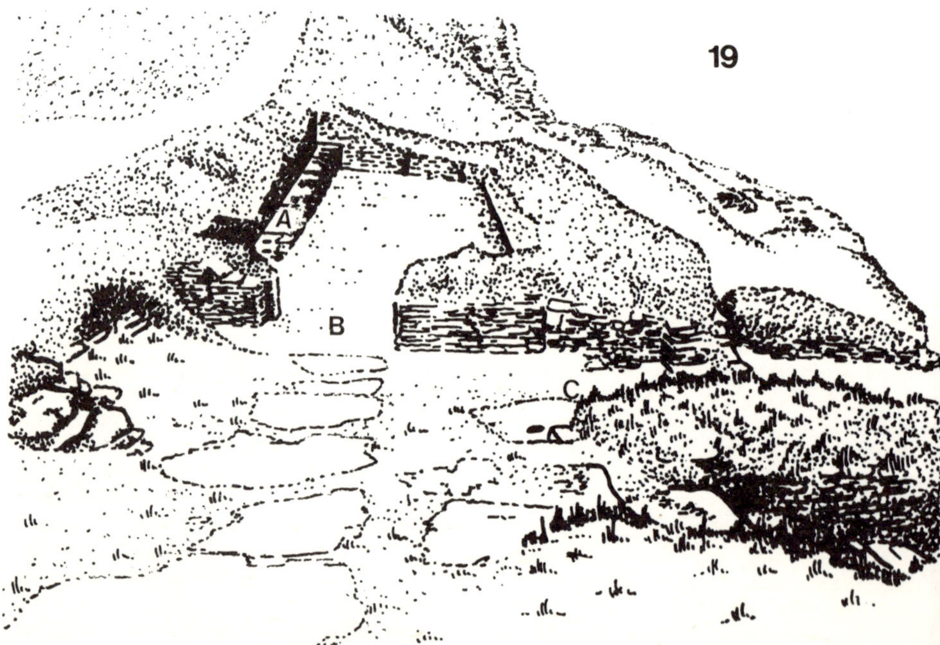


19

▲ The long room had an internal bench **A**, double doors **B**, heavy stone floor and open ended annexes **C**. It may, therefore, have been the scriptorium where the monks could read and copy books. The annexes would have given more light to the users than the main room.

20

▲ Beneath the floor of this building were a number of channels, eg **A**. They may have been drains or, less likely, a debased form of hypocaust. The idea of a hypocaust and the apparent existence of steam baths **18** are, however, at odds with the austerity which the siting of the buildings **16A** implies. Indeed some have questioned whether the buildings were monastic. If not they must represent the buildings of nobility and one is tempted to recall Geoffrey of Monmouth's association of the site with an Arthurian Duke. On the other hand it is not known what creature comforts, if any, the monks allowed the sons of nobility in their charge. In addition to those sons there might be older members of a royal family in residence, for at least two contemporary kings lived in monasteries elsewhere. Whatever the interpretation, the remains suggest Roman style comforts were enjoyed after AD 400. Certainly by that time there was a strong tradition of constructing rectangular, rather than circular buildings.

*The castle utilised the natural defences offered by the site and, consequently, has an odd plan. Much of its present character is the work of Earl Richard, younger brother of Henry III and from the late fourteenth century functioned as a state prison. By the sixteenth century it was a ruin. The earliest structures, however, belong to the fifth century and have been interpreted as a monastery. Despite the date and Mediterranean links of the latter, there is no evidence for an Arthurian association. Geoffrey of Monmouth, who in the twelfth century was the first to link the site with Arthur, would have known about the foundations newly discovered in building the castle chapel. He also knew that the scenery was spectacular and the owners powerful patrons; the latter particularly important to anyone like Geoffrey. Geoffrey could not avoid putting the site in his story, yet he did not make it Camelot. It was the home of Ygerna the beautiful wife of Gorlois, Duke of Cornwall, whom Arthur's father Uther Pendragon seduced by deceit (changing into the shape of Gorlois) and treachery. Geoffrey's Tintagel Arthur is thus somewhat different from the later medieval and Hollywood myths. Lust, wars resulting from lust, and shape changing are recurrent elements in Celtic stories. From such stories – surely the ancient book Geoffrey refers to – he culled or invented his Arthur.*

**15 RESTORMEL CASTLE**
SX 104614

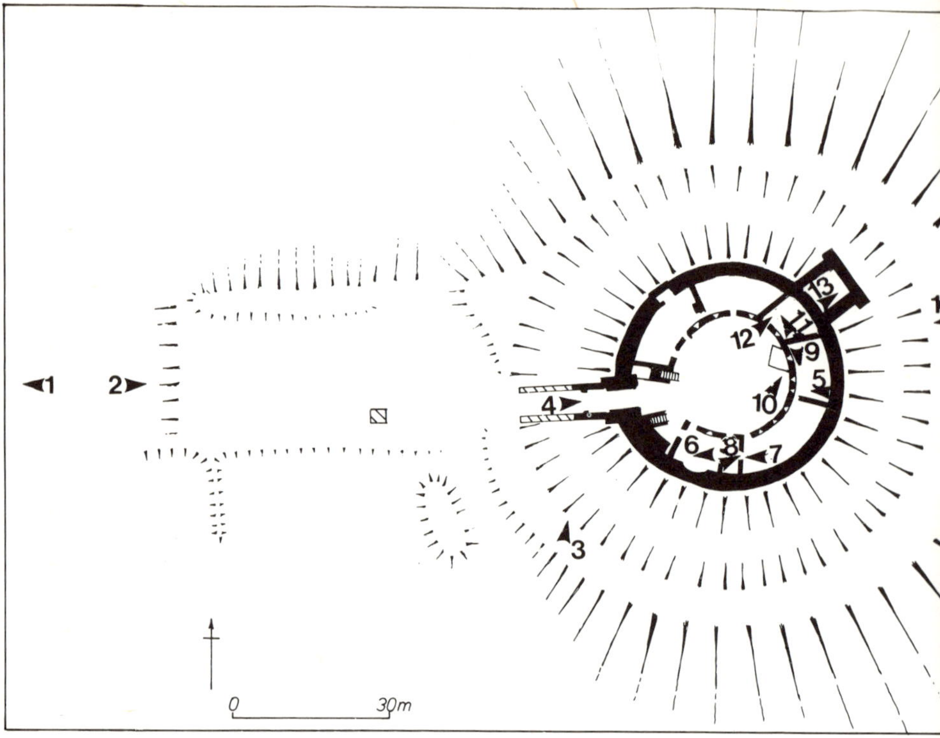


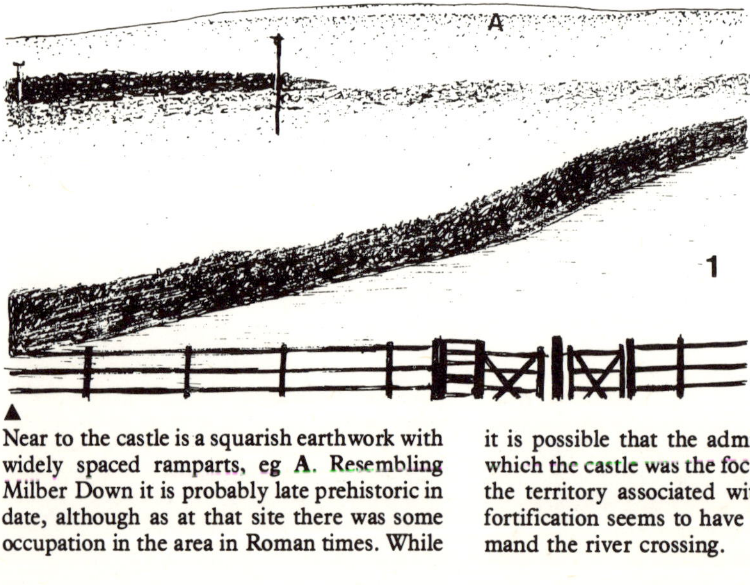


▲
Near to the castle is a squarish earthwork with widely spaced ramparts, eg **A**. Resembling Milber Down it is probably late prehistoric in date, although as at that site there was some occupation in the area in Roman times. While it is possible that the administrative unit for which the castle was the focus had its origins in the territory associated with **A** the medieval fortification seems to have been sited to command the river crossing.

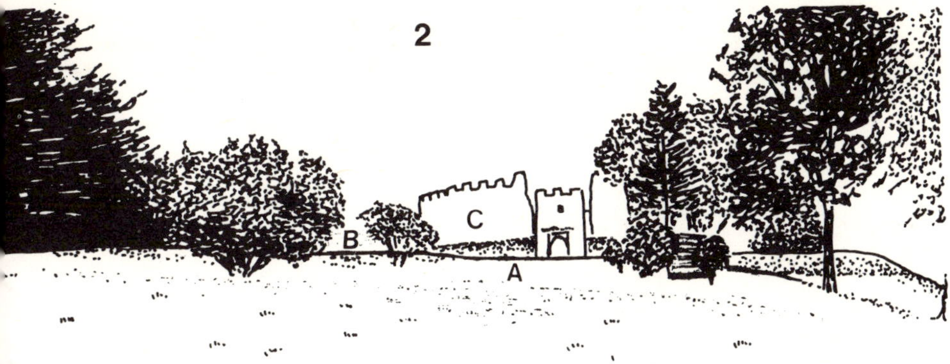


▲ The building of the castle must have taken place long before the first reference in 1264, for its plan — a ringwork and bailey — was obsolete by the thirteenth century. The bailey **A** was enclosed by a timber topped rampart **B** but the ringwork was replaced by the present stone structure **C**. Stone foundations have been detected within **A** and some must be the buildings referred to in a survey of 1337: hall, chapel, chambers and kitchen.

▲ The original ringwork and its buildings was protected by a rampart built with material from ditch **A**. The stone curtain **B** which replaced the presumed palisade was inserted into the back of that rampart, so the front of the latter has survived **C** — hence the ditch side there is much higher than at **D**. As at Exeter castle the earth and timber ringwork had a stone gate tower. The vertical ends of the curtain wall and later gatetower extension **E** are where those walls were butted against that first stone tower at **F**. The bridge **G** is itself built against **E**.

4

◀ At **A** are the remains of the outer arch of the original gatetower. The square recess **B** suggests that there may have been a drawbridge between the inner and the outer arches and above the passageway was a room entered from the stairs at **C**.

5

▲
The stone stairs **A** were roofed by timbers on corbels **B**. Steps **C** led to an area higher than the rest of the battlements, but whether that was the roof of the old gatetower **3F** or a platform above that tower is not clear, but there were no corresponding stairs at **D**. The sloping wall top **E** was probably to protect those on **C**, rather than part of a gable for a roof. The pitch of the contemporary roofs can be seen at **F** and was steeper than **E**.

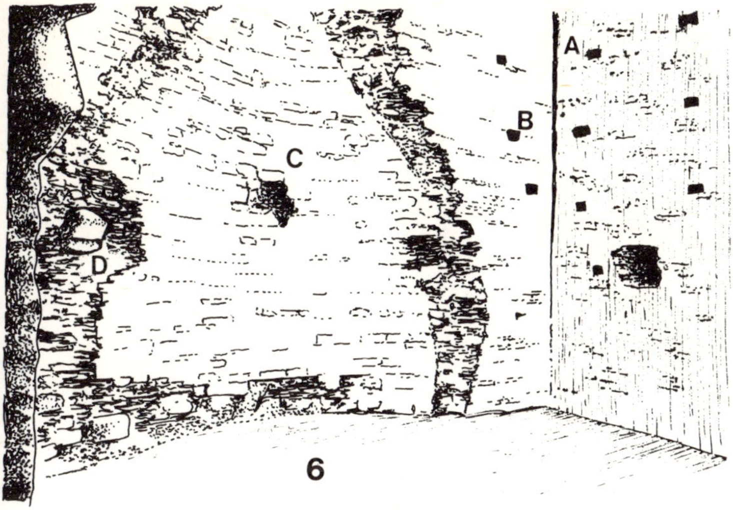


▲ The internal buildings were butted **A** against the curtain showing that the latter was built first, if only by a short time. The holes **B** are for scaffolding. The timbers were placed spiral fashion, not vertically, and the holes later plugged with plaster. This room, with the great fireplace **C**, was the kitchen. Corbel **D** is all that remains of the great hood.

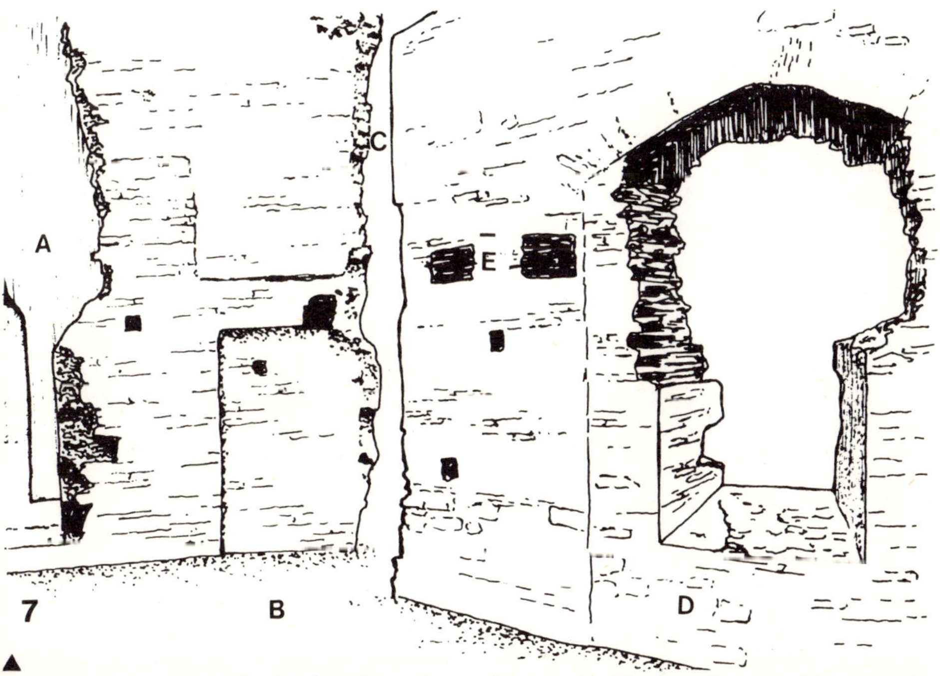


▲ A pantry **A** separated the kitchen from the great hall **B**. The hall was at first floor level and had an external staircase reached through a door at **C**. Blocked doorway **D** cannot be contemporary for it cut across the floor of the hall which was supported by beams, eg **E**.

▲

The roof of the hall was supported by two principal trusses **A** and **B**. Centrally placed between the two windows **C** and **D** was the fireplace **E**. It seems to have had a hood and stone hearth supported by corbelling **F** and **G**. The dais, as usual, was at the opposite end to the kitchen, door **H** leading from there to the solar. ▶

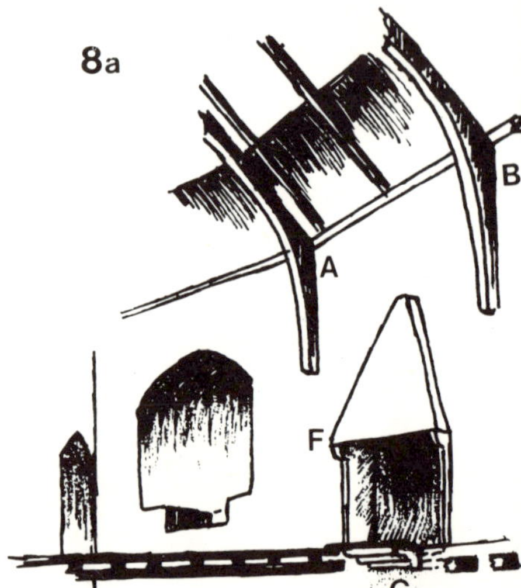

◀ The door into the solar had an arch springing from **A**. The room, which had its own fireplace **B**, was roofed like the great hall: a truss **C** with lateral members on corbels **D**. A private staircase **E** led to the battlements, while the ground floor and its pit **F** were for storage.

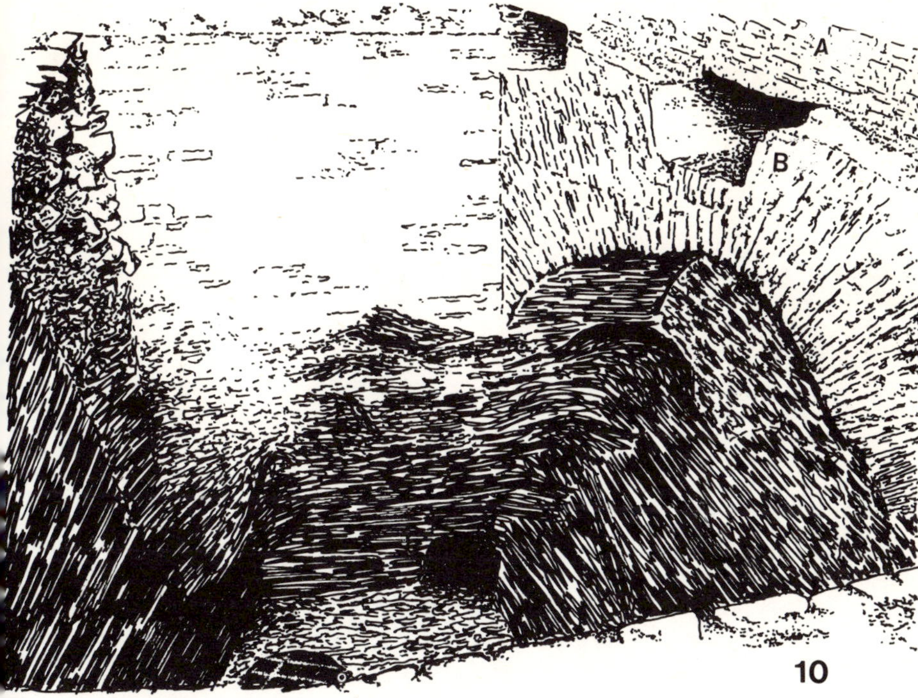


10

▲ The wall of the solar **A** was built at an angle over the wellpit of the earlier castle. The pit seems to have had a cover resting on beam **B**.

The bed chamber was heated by fireplace **A**. It was later modified by the addition of an oven **B**. ▼

11

Another modification was the addition of the chapel; the different masonry **A** and **B** results from the arch being inserted in a hole knocked through the earlier wall **A**. ▶

12

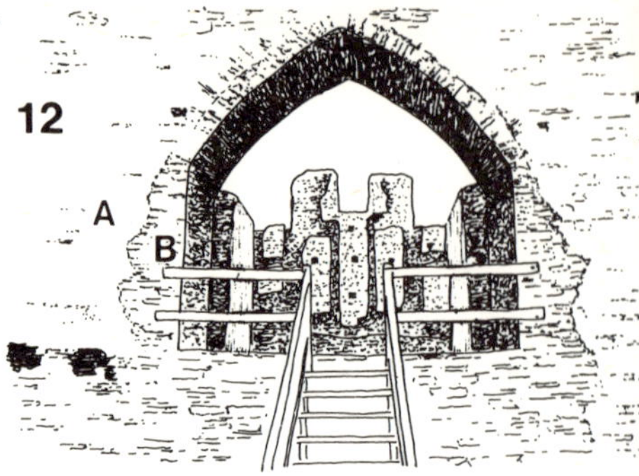


*The masonry castle represents the reconstruction of an earlier ringwork and bailey structure. The first castle was largely of earth and timber with a stone gatetower, which was incorporated in the later building. The latter was itself subsequently modified, principally by the addition of the chapel.*

13

▲
The floor of the chapel has been sloped to allow drainage; originally it was level as can be seen at **A**. There was a window **B** in each side wall and one above the altar at **C**. Although subsequently blocked with masonry reinforced by timbers **D**, the sides of window **C** can still be traced at **E**. To one side of the altar was the piscina **F**. Blocked doorway **G**, with its moulded jamb **H**, led to the priest's room.

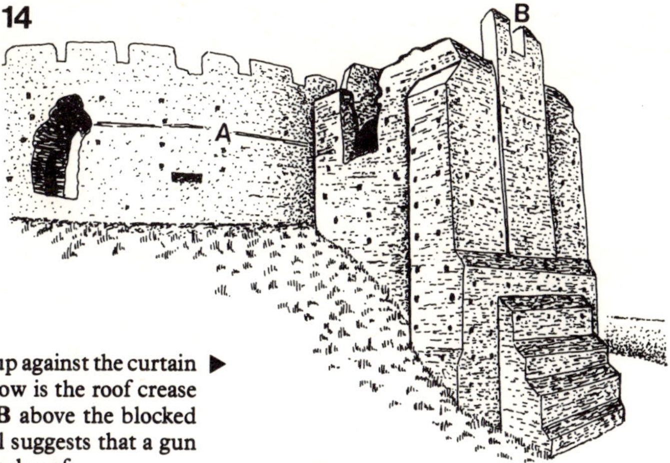


The priest's room butted up against the curtain ▶ and all that can be seen now is the roof crease **A**. The high battlement **B** above the blocked east window of the chapel suggests that a gun was mounted on the chapel roof.

## 16 The Tristan Stone
SX112524

The stone, which stands in a modern base, ▶ carries a sixth-century inscription: [?] Hic Iacit Cunomori — 'here lies . . . son of Cunomorus'. The missing name is said to have been Drustanus the earlier form of Tristan. Tristan was associated in medieval romance with King Arthur, but in Welsh stories he was linked with another hero, Mark. This is interesting for a ninth-century life of St Paul Aurelian speaks of 'King Mark, who is also called by another name Cunomorus', and a twelfth-century version of the Trisan story calls Mark's castle Lancien, a name which seems to be perpetuated in *Lantyan*, a farm 4km north of here. 2km to the north is Castle Dore, a prehistoric 'fort' which has also produced evidence of post-Roman occupation and more specifically building arrangements which might be those of a lord or petty king. Yet although all the evidence seems to hang together it is suspect, for in Welsh tradition Tristan was the son of Tallwch, not Cunomorus, and Mark was a hero of Glamorgan not Cornwall. Further, Gildas writing in the sixth century says Cunomorus or Kynwawr was succeeded as king of Dumnonia by Constantine. It seems, therefore, that the twelfth-century author of the romance knew of the Welsh stories, of this inscription, and the local geography and archaeology and welded them together — unfortunately incorrectly.

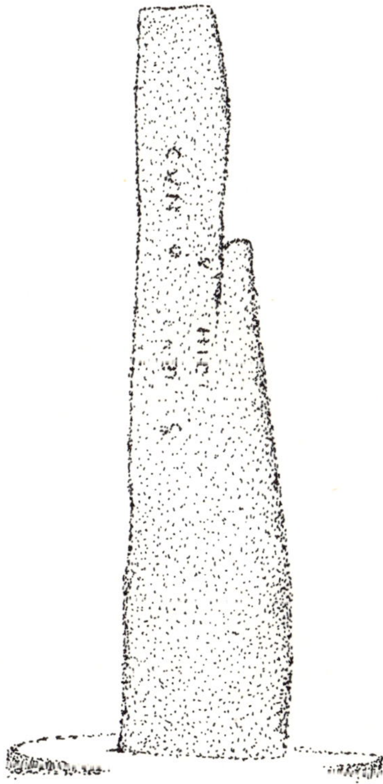

*The Arthurian romance was woven from a variety of material and some of the personages were translated from South Wales into Cornwall.*

## 17 Fowey and Polruan
SX 123511

▲
In 1450 a French fleet forced its way into Fowey Harbour which was the principal port of south Cornwall. The local response was the construction of two towers either side of the entrance with a chain stretched between the two. That in Fowey **A** is ruined. The front and most of the sides have gone but the arrangements seem to have been very similar to those at Polruan. A map of 1540 depicts a drawbridge linking **A** to the cliff behind and implies, by the number of cannon mounted, that it was the principal tower of the two.

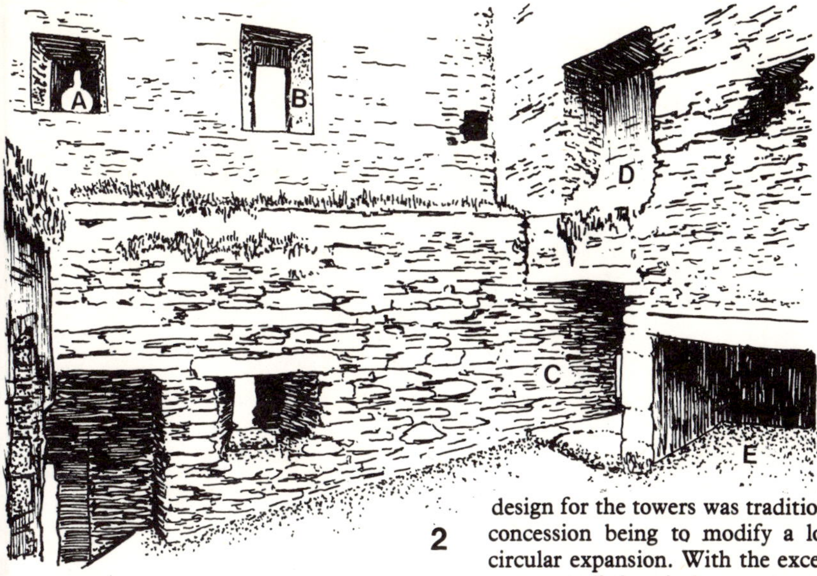


2

▲ Even though both towers had small cannon they were essentially fortified guard rooms at either end of the chain. Cannons were still relatively new in 1450 and, consequently, the design for the towers was traditional, the only concession being to modify a loop **A** by a circular expansion. With the exception of the gun port all the windows were equipped with heavy shutters in rebates, eg **B**, and the largest windows, eg **C**, were placed on the landward side. Each floor was served by a fireplace **D** and **E** suggesting a permanent, if small, garrison.

3

▲ The staircase to the battlements **A** was separated from that to the first floor **B**, so the latter could no doubt be sealed in emergency. The position of loop **C** suggests that the ground outside was lower and the approach narrower than today.

▲
In the reign of Henry VIII the defences were added to by the building of St Catherine's Castle **A**. Less sophisticated than either St Mawes or Pendennis, which it preceded, it nevertheless shows the advances made by Henry's time: larger ordnance, true gunports and curved walls. In the nineteenth century a new battery **B** was built.

*The earliest coastal defences were built on local initiative and with little concession to the new, but still unreliable, weapons. In Henry VIII's reign the government took a direct role in coastal defence and built a series of forts specially designed for cannon warfare.*

## 18 King Doniert's Stone
SX 236688

The tops of the two stones have mortices for attaching shafts for they were both cross bases. The inscription reads DONIERT ROGAVIT PRO ANIMA — 'Doniert asks for spirit [life]'. Doniert is Durngarth son of Caraduc the King of Cornwall, who was drowned about AD 873. The precise reason for the use of two crosses and the inscription is not known, but as the inscribed stone was displaced in 1685 it is possible the two originally faced each other. Paired crosses are rare, usually ninth to tenth century, and apparently funerary.

▶

*In the ninth century Cornwall was still an independent kingdom albeit under Anglo-Saxon hegemony.*

## 19 The Hurlers and Rillaton Barrow
SX 258714 and SX 260719

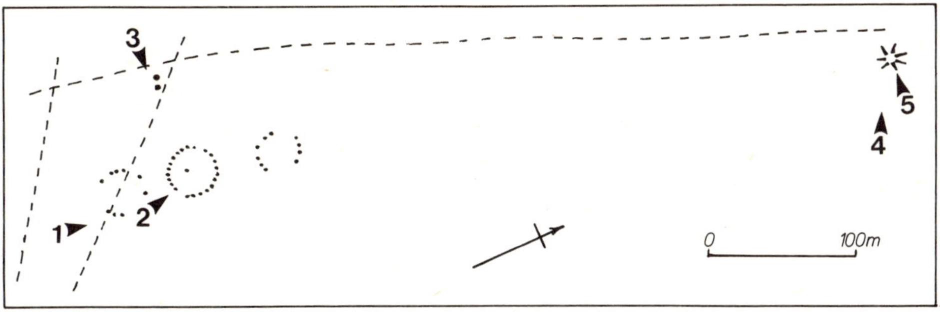

▲
The Hurlers are three stone circles **A**, **B** and **C**. In the late sixteenth century the locals believed the stones 'had been men sometime transformed into stones for profaning the Lord's Day with hurling the ball'. The circles are almost in line and that axis, if extended, points to the hilltop and Rillaton Barrow **D**. Excavations in 1936 found that the area between the circles, the south side of **B** and the interior of **C** had been roughly paved.

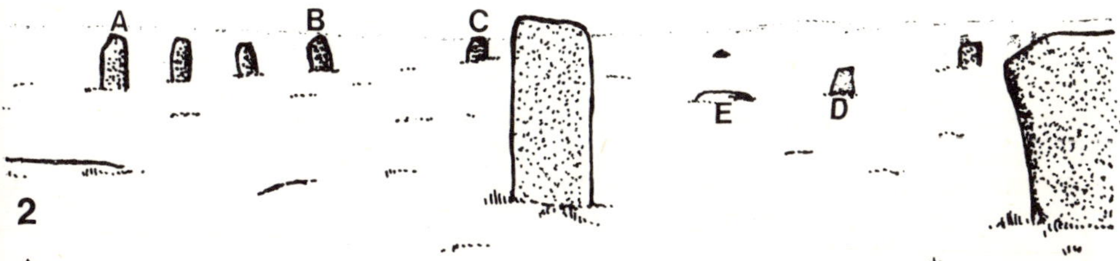


▲
The excavations also revealed a pit within this circle, and evidence for the stones having been hammered smoother and erected with their tops approximately level, eg between **A** and **B**. At Stonehenge the stones were also hammer dressed, while the pit and pavements are features repeated in circles elsewhere, in contexts which can be dated to the late Neolithic-Early Bronze Age. In such sites, as here, there is evidence for at least one entrance — the wider space between stones **B** and **C** and there may have been another on the opposite side of the circle. The two 'entrances' are not diametrically opposed but lines at right angles to them intersect near stone **D**, which is not in the centre of the circle. It is possible **D** was paired with **E**.

3

▲
Certainly paired stones like these are often near or associated with stone circles (the other nearby standing stones are later boundary markers). Perhaps predictably these two are called the Pipers, the two men who encouraged with music those engaged in 'hurling'. It is unlikely that the stones were used for astronomical sightings from the circles, as their orientation does not fall along any radial line. Looking along the stones, for example, it will be seen that their axis, if extended, would be a tangent of the central circle. Paired stones can in fact be a class of monument by themselves and are perhaps related to, or derived from, similar arrangements beneath Neolithic barrows.

Neolithic barrows are normally thought of as being 'long' or rectangular, but a not insignificant number are round like those of the Bronze Age. As a rule of thumb the Neolithic round barrows tend to be the larger and this one might be of that period. Its present shape is the result of nineteenth-century excavations. They showed that the mound was made of turf and stone, and that high up at **A** was an Early Bronze Age cist.
▼

4

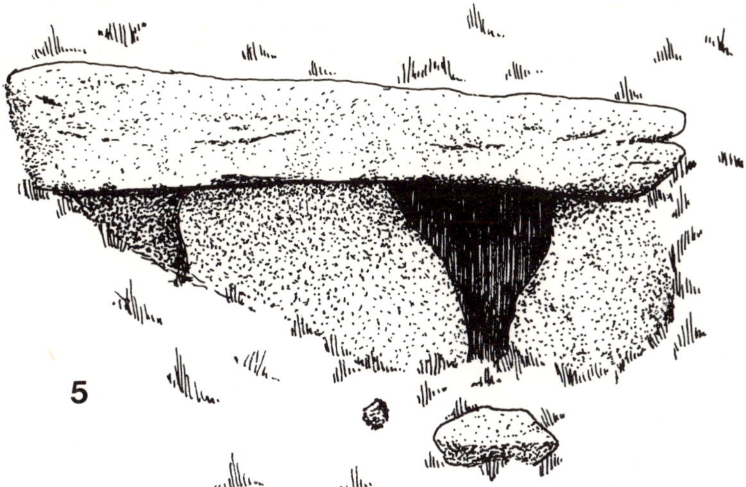

5

▲
The large cist can only have been constructed after the rest of the mound, showing that the latter was very early Bronze Age or, more likely, Neolithic. Within the cist was an extended skeleton, a gold cup, a dagger, some pieces of 'ivory', 'glass' beads and pottery. All but the cup have been lost but the 'ivory' was probably bone and the 'glass', faience, a glass-like substance made in the Eastern Mediterranean and traded in Western Europe for raw materials such as tin. Those trading links are further emphasised by the gold cup. Its overall shape, decoration on the handle and diamond shaped washers can be paralleled in a gold cup from Bonn, Germany, and in Mycenae in the East Mediterranean/Aegean. The same shape and decoration also occurs in two shale cups from the Farway necropolis east of Exeter The identity of the individual buried here can never be known but like a number of contemporaries in Wessex he had amassed or been given a small fortune to accompany him to the next world.

> *By the Early Bronze Age trade contacts stretched as far as the East Mediterranean, and as in more recent centuries the 'more civilised' traded glass bangles and beads with the 'less civilised'. There is no evidence that the stone circles were used for astronomical alignments but they were carefully constructed. The origins of Early Bronze Age sites seem to lie in the Neolithic.*

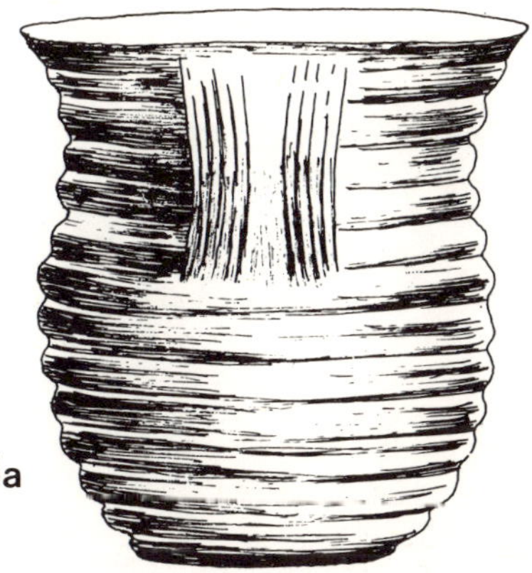

5a

▲
*Gold cup now in British Museum*

5b

▲
*Shale cup from Faraway, now in Rougemont House Museum, Exeter*

## 20 Trethevy Quoit
SX 259689

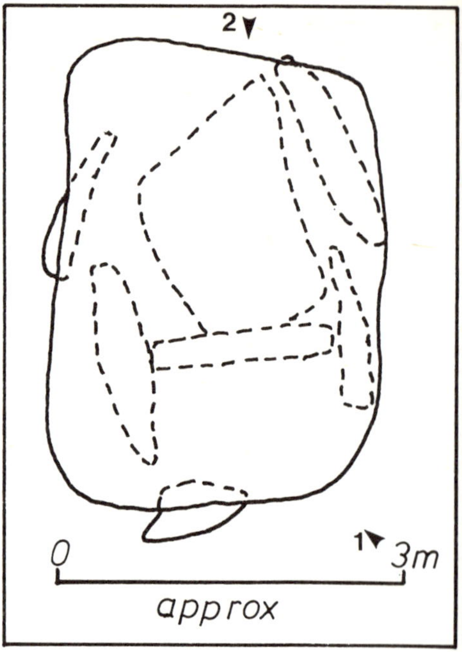


A small opening **A** led from the antechamber **B** into the main chamber. There are no known finds from the chamber and most of the cairn **C** has been destroyed. The mound or cairn is said to have been oval in plan, although that is no longer readily apparent, nor can its original height be known. It is quite possible that the mound top was flush with the capstone. The natural hole **D** may have been the reason for that stone's selection.

The shape of the side stones at **A** shows that the square opening between the two chambers **1C** was also natural. The small holes **B** are relatively modern, having been drilled for blasting. Originally the stone would have stood upright.

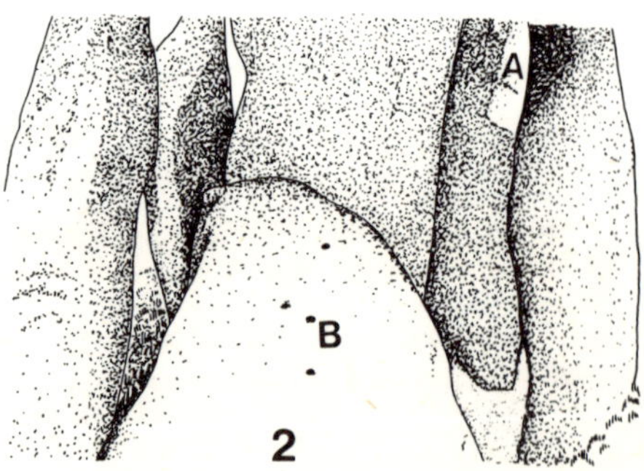


*The tomb, which was within a mound, consisted of a main chamber with a small one in front. By analogy with sites elsewhere it was probably used in the later Neolithic-Early Bronze Age.*

## 21 Lewannick Church
SX 276807

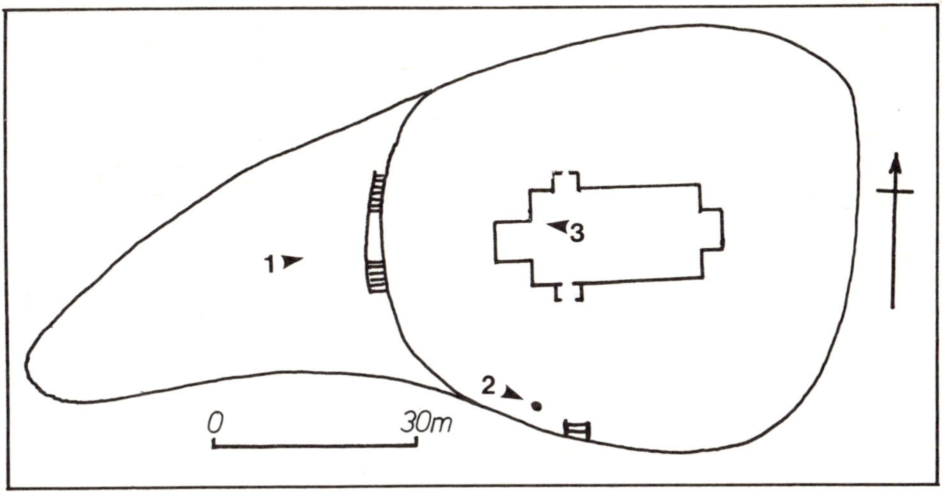


Circular churchyards like this one are representatives of a tradition going back at least to the fifth century AD. Continuous use over the centuries has led to an accumulation of material inside the perimeter, so that its surface is now above that of the surrounding area. In Old Cornish the word for such areas was *Lann* or *Lan*, an element in the twelfth-century name of Lewannick—*Lan*wenuc. Whether there was an early church here is not known, but two 'gravestones' have survived.

▼

1

2

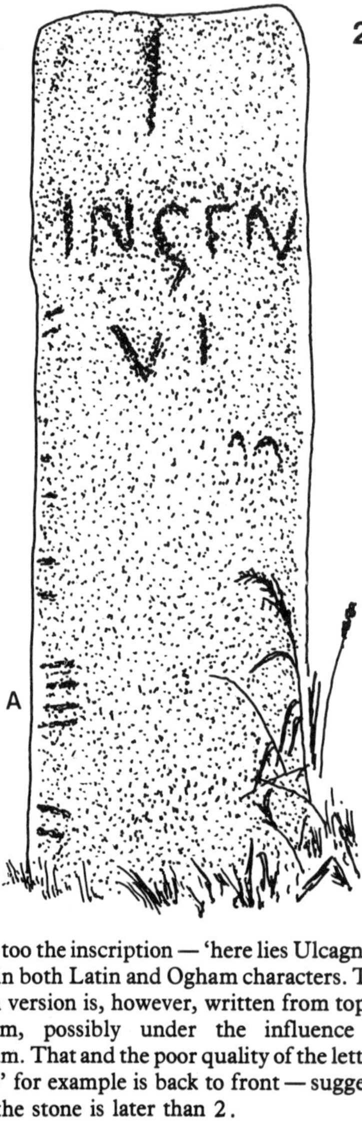


◀ The original focal point of the graveyard may have been this stone, for it carries the inscription INGENVI MEMORIA and the word *memoria* seems to have meant 'the special grave'. The term has been found on only two other stones in Britain, but is common in North Africa suggesting that links were maintained with that area in the sixth century. The latter date for this example is suggested by the Ogham translation down the side **A**. The Ogham alphabet was developed in southern Ireland, probably as a result of contact with the Roman world, and consisted of twenty letters or symbols arranged either side of a line. As such it readily utilised the edges of standing stones.

3

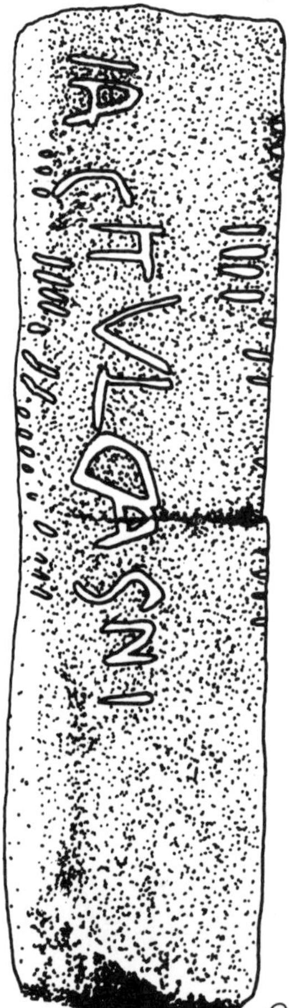

Here too the inscription — 'here lies Ulcagnus' ▶ — is in both Latin and Ogham characters. The Latin version is, however, written from top to bottom, possibly under the influence of Ogham. That and the poor quality of the letters — 'D' for example is back to front — suggests that the stone is later than 2.

*Contact with the Mediterranean world was not broken by the 'departure' of the Romans, but there was also a strong Irish influence in the area in the sixth century.*

*Ogham alphabet*
▼

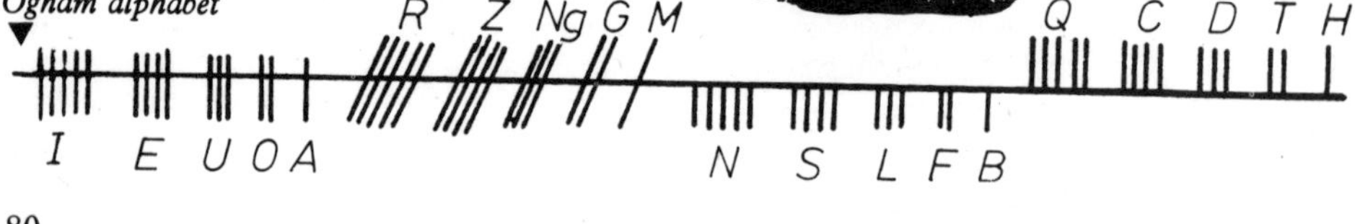

SX331846

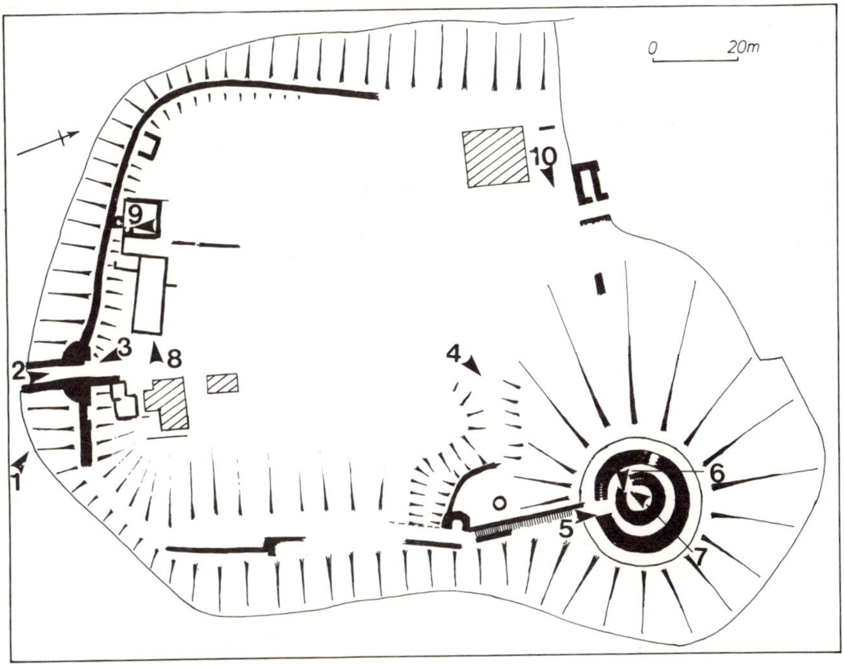

▲ Launceston and Trematon near Plymouth were the only castles in Cornwall in existence at the time of the Domesday Survey. Both were held by Robert of Mortain and were probably built in, or shortly after, 1068 when an expedition left Exeter to put down rebellion. The stone structure is later, but has been strongly influenced by the first construction which consisted of a motte **A** and bailey **B**. The motte must have been capped by a wooden tower or building, while the bailey ramparts, later replaced by the stone curtain wall **C**, were timber fronted. Robert's castle was built on a natural ridge, perhaps in or adjacent to a hillfort, for in the Domesday Book it is called *Dun*heved and earlier occupation was found beneath the ramparts. The town, with its own wall and gates, developed after the building of the castle. Town and castle were separated by ditch **D**.

The principal entrance was reached by a bridge ▶ across the ditch. Most of the bridge was demolished and the ground outside lowered for road improvement but one (blocked up) arch **A** remains. The carriageway must have been of timber resting on an offset at **B**. The high walls either side of that carriageway made the bridge a barbican, confining attackers while subjecting them to fire from the gatehouse. The entrance passage itself was flanked by towers with rounded fronts, a moulded course **C** and splayed base **D**. The stone bridge is built against that base and may have replaced a drawbridge. The occurrence of moulding like **C** on most of the other structures indicates that much of the stone castle was built at the same time in the mid thirteenth century, probably by Richard of Cornwall who held it for the king.

2

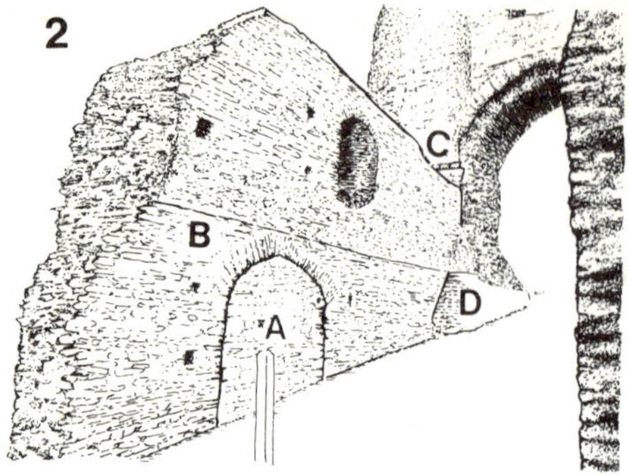


3

▲
The gates were protected by a portcullis in slot **A** and the passageway originally ended at **B**. The buildings butted against the gatehouse at **B** have been built with stones, eg **C**, from structures demolished elsewhere. There were frequent repairs. In 1337 and 1353, for example, the foundations of the curtain wall were damaged by the pigs of the townfolk rooting in the moat.

4

▲
When first built the motte was surrounded by a circular ditch **A**. The development of gate-tower **B** and the construction of terrace **C** to contain and protect a well on the inner side of that ditch led to a new ditch **D**. The new bridge was of wood supported by a massive timber in chaser **E** and the half nearest **B** was probably a drawbridge. It was replaced by a stone one supported from **F** and **G**. The bridge was rebuilt on a number of occasions and finally replaced by a causeway in the eighteenth century. The stairs up the motte were protected by a building with a leaded roof. The height of its walls can be seen at **H**. The gate-tower and keep have a moulded course **I** and **J** like **2C**.

5

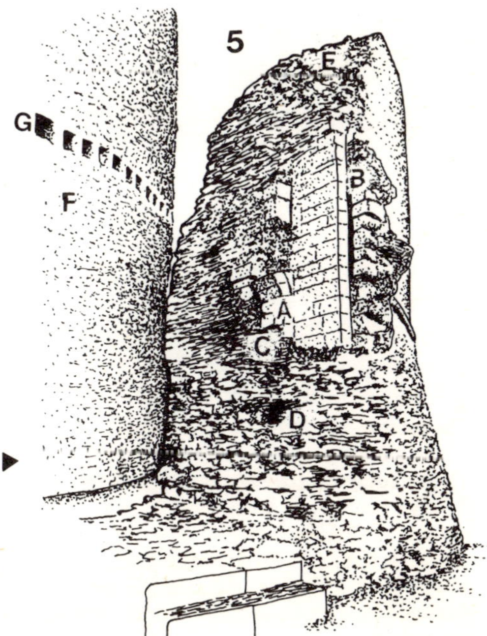


The arched entrance of the keep **A** was defended by a portcullis in slot **B** and a door secured by two drawbars **C** and **D**. Originally there was only a shell keep with internal buildings against wall **E**. Later the buildings were demolished and tower **F** constructed. The space between the two was roofed on joists **G**. ▶

The ground floor room of the new tower had a ▶ door secured on the outside by drawbar **A**. That and the lack of any windows suggests that the room was either for storage or a prison.

By contrast, the room above was purely domestic. It had a window with seats on either side **A** and a fireplace **B** with a hood carried on corbels **C**. Corbel **D** supported the single beam for the wooden floor while others like **E** were for the roof members.
▼

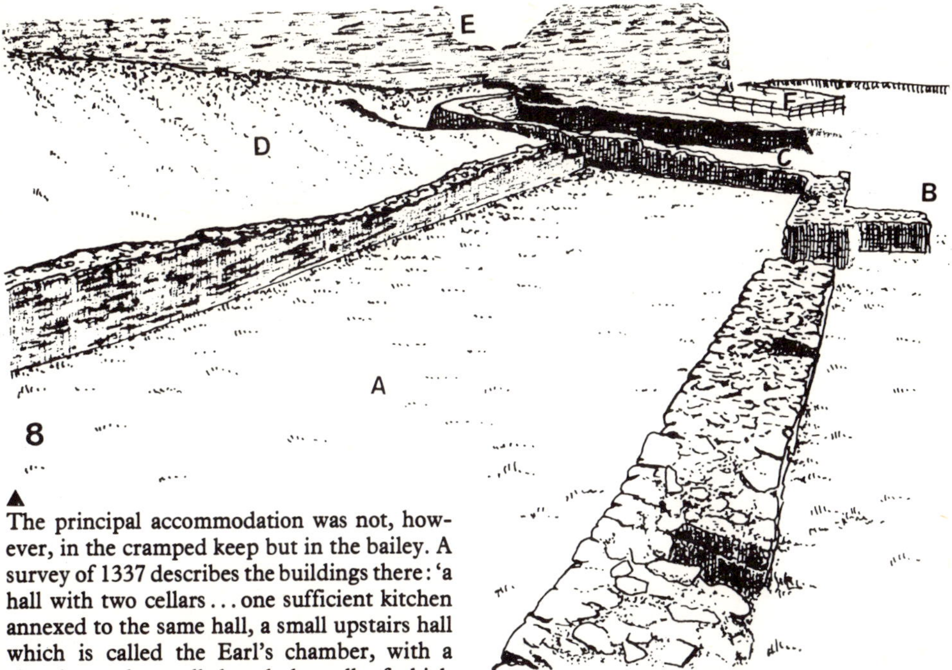


8

▲ The principal accommodation was not, however, in the cramped keep but in the bailey. A survey of 1337 describes the buildings there: 'a hall with two cellars . . . one sufficient kitchen annexed to the same hall, a small upstairs hall which is called the Earl's chamber, with a chamber and a small chapel, the walls of which are of timber and plank . . . one old and feeble small hall with a chamber and a cellar convenient for the Constable, and one little new kitchen annexed . . . one chapel in good order . . . two stables sufficient for ten horses; one gaol . . . and one other prison called the Larder . . .' An 'assize hall' is recorded 1201 and Leland in 1539 refers to one 'for syses and sessions'. The latter has been tentatively identified with **A** while the great hall was at right angles at **B**. 80 ft (24 m) long and with a central hearth, it had been constructed on a layer of clay dumped over the demolished remains of earlier buildings. At the south end was a kitchen **C** cut into the back of the first earth and timber rampart **D**. That rampart must have been kept in use until the building of the stone curtain **E** in the thirteenth century. Some time before, however, a series of stone towers, eg **F**, had been constructed.

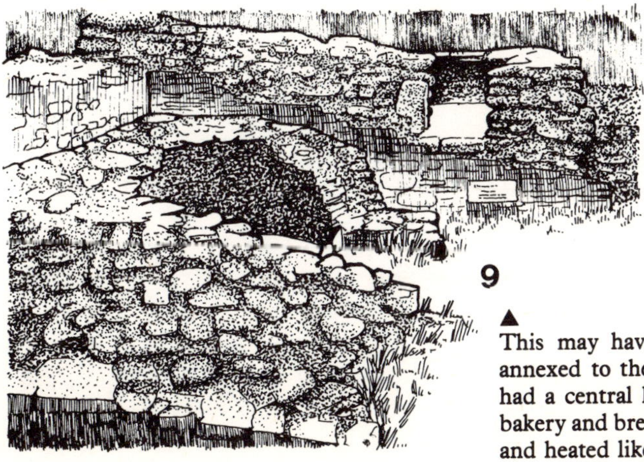

9

▲ This may have been the 'sufficient kitchen annexed to the . . . hall' of 1337. Originally it had a central hearth, but was converted to a bakery and brewhouse. The ovens were domed and heated like those at Okehampton **8**.

▲
The north gate was not as important as the southern one and may be slightly later in date. It seems to have been built against one of the early rampart towers like **9F** and part **A** was later used to hold George Fox. The same room may have been one of the prisons referred to in 1337. From the gate the curtain **B** continued up the side of the motte.

*The thirteenth-century stone castle replaced, but was strongly influenced by, the early Norman motte and bailey one. Within the bailey were the principal buildings while the motte was crowned by a modified shell keep approached by covered stairs and defended by a portcullis, inner gate and drawbridge.*

## 23 COTEHELE
SX 423686

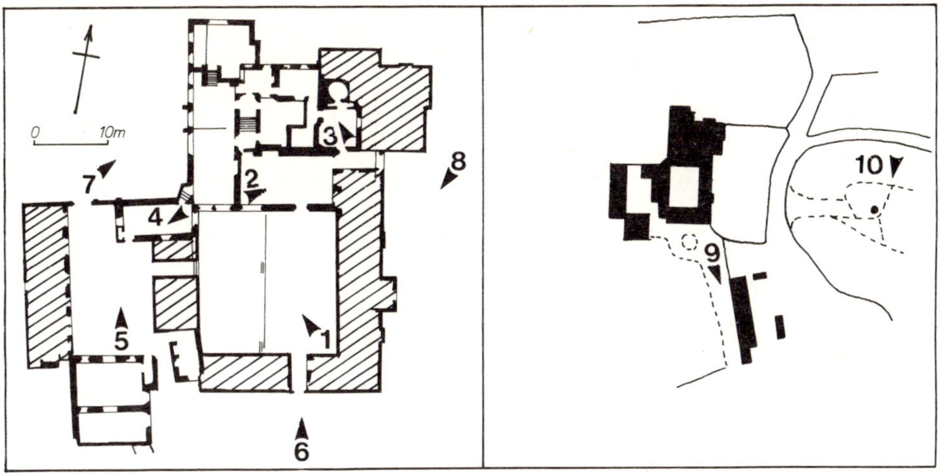

▲ The buildings ranged around the principal courtyard consist of the hall **A**, chapel **B**, accommodation and offices. Although the building appears at first to be a single design, various modifications are apparent. The masonry of the chapel, for example, is different from that of range **C** while the stonework above and below windows **D** shows them to be an insertion. Gable **E** also appears to be an insertion, for it is built against the moulding of the chapel roof and there is a vertical break in the stonework at **F**. Again, the large blocks **G** suggest that the hall itself has been raised in height. This may be the work of Sir Piers Edgcumbe (who died in 1539), for the windows associated with **G** carry heraldry connected with his wife and the hoods are very similar to those over the windows at Berry Pomeroy. There they seem to belong to a building begun after 1540.

▲
The possibility that the present hall is of two periods would help explain the existence of the Tudor style fireplace, doors and windows while the three doors at **A** are typical of the screens passage of a (earlier) medieval hall. In a typical medieval hall the lord's dais would be at the opposite end to the screens passage and again this is echoed here in the position of the fireplace, the large window and the door to the principal suite of rooms **B**. The Tudor architecture can be attributed to Sir Piers Edgcumbe (**1G**), his father or both, but the date of the earlier building is uncertain. It is possible it represents work begun in the traditional manner by Sir Piers' father, Richard, after he was knighted at the Battle of Bosworth in 1485, but is more likely to be earlier.

Attached to the principal suite of rooms was ▶ the chapel with its 'original' tiled floor **A**. The clock **B** was erected by Sir Richard Edgcumbe in 1485-9. The chapel was, however, not just for the family, door **C** allowing estate workers to enter from the outer court. The use of the chapel by such people may have been the reason for the provision of a window between it and the private suite.

The chapel belfry **A**, in a style characteristic of the later fifteenth century, contained two bells, one for the clock **5B** and the other for church services. The chapel itself may, in part, be that dedicated as newly built in 1411 and must be part of the pre-1485 house. That house must, like its successor, have been built around a courtyard for the passageway through **B** was intended to be closed and defended; a combined loop and gunport **C** being provided.
▼

◀ The kitchen was equipped with large fireplaces for cooking and provided with a great oven **A**. This was heated by lighting a fire inside. The embers were then withdrawn and the food inserted.

6

▲
At a time contemporary with the heightening of the hall (**1G**) a new entrance **A** was provided. The passageway and its tower was built with large blocks like **1G** quite different from the masonry **B** of the earlier building.

7

7a

▲
◀ Evidence for raising the height of the hall block can again be seen above and below **A**. A moulded course **B** preserved at **C** indicates that the heightened building had a roof pitch different from the existing one **D**. The pitch of **D** is the same as gable **E** (**1E**), so the latter is indeed a later modification, perhaps connected with the building of tower **F** in 1627. The old building ended at **G**.

▲
The eastern range was altered in the nineteenth century by the addition of **A**. The original masonry can be seen at **B**.

The house was the centre of an estate, for the wealth of the owners was derived from the land. The size of this barn is an indication of the size of the estate. Further away, sited where there was adequate power, were the mill and forge. A quay was built to allow produce to be shipped out and lime kilns provided the means to improve the land. ▶

The fishpond **A** and dovecot **B** are a reminder that despite the wealth of the inhabitants fresh red meat was scarce in winter and had to be supplemented. ▶

*The present house, which was the centre of a large estate, is primarily in Tudor style. There have been many minor alterations but it appears to represent an adaption and re-building of an earlier fifteenth-century structure.*

**24 Lydford**
SX510848

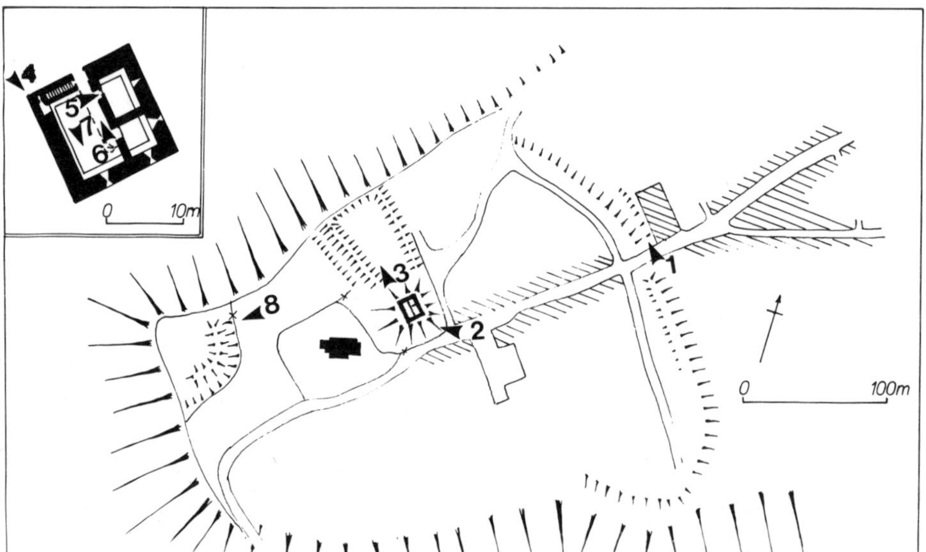

In the late ninth century, under severe pressure from Danish armies, King Alfred created a number of *burghs* or fortified towns. There were four in Devon — Exeter, Halwell near Totnes, Pitton near or at Barnstaple and Lydford. Here a steep sided spur was fortified by a rampart **A**. Where it crossed the spur and there were no protecting slopes a ditch **B** was added. At first the rampart was a turf wall revetted with boulders, but later it was strengthened with a core of rubble and mortar. The value of the defences was proved in 997 when the Danish army 'harried both in Cornwall, Wales and Devon... and entered the estuary of the Tamar, and so up it until they came to Lydford....' (Anglo-Saxon Chronicle). It is probable that the present main street was also the principle Saxon one, and the evidence suggests that the town was laid out either side of that lane. Some of the present side lanes and building plots may thus be direct descendants of those founded by King Alfred. Between Ethelred II and Edward the Confessor the town had its own mint issuing silver pennies and later it became a stannery town.

The church **A** is dedicated to St Petrock, a Celtic rather than Saxon saint, suggesting there was some form of settlement in the area prior to Alfred's *burgh*. Excavation showed the castle was built on the site of former houses, but whether they were deliberately demolished or already abandoned is unclear. The Domesday book noted that forty houses had been laid waste since 1066, possibly as a result of the crushing of rebellion. The tower rising above its motte **B** and the round headed windows **C** indicate a twelfth-century date for the castle, but it is not until 1194-5 that there is a reference to a fortified building, and that a prison.
▼

2

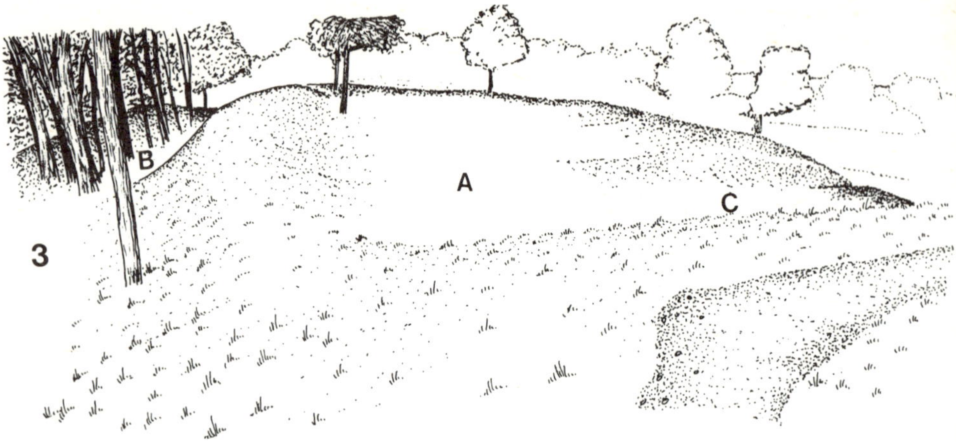


▲
Behind the motte was a bailey **A** protected by a rampart and ditch **B** on three sides. The rampart did not continue in front of the motte, but the latter was surrounded by a ditch. Excavation at **C** showed the bailey bank to have been carried across that ditch, so the motte must have been constructed earlier if only by a short time.

▲
The tower is largely of two periods, the upper part **A** being built on earlier, thicker walls **B**. Arch **C** dates the building of **A** to the thirteenth century. The door was secured by two drawbars **D**.

The inside of the tower was subdivided into two areas by wall **A** and the northern half further subdivided. The smallest room **B** was secured from the outside by drawbar **C**, while beneath its floor was a 'cellar'. There can thus be little doubt the tower was the prison referred to in medieval documents and the 'cellar' was the pit used for the most unfortunate of prisoners. In 1510 it was described by one who had been briefly secured there as 'one of the most anncious, contagious and detestable places wythen this realme'. ▶

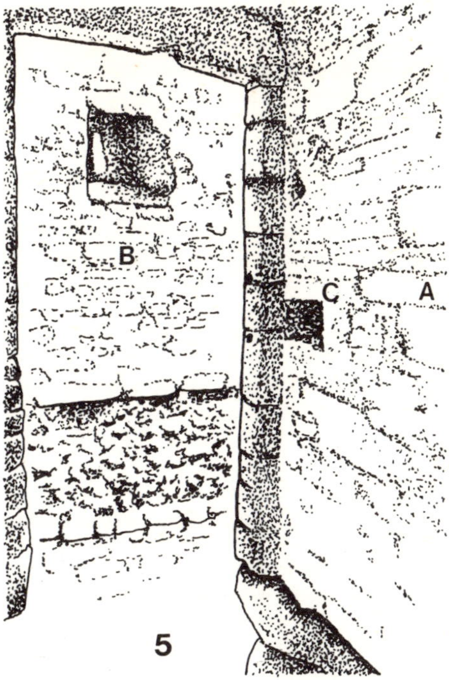


5

6

◀ The evidence from here and elsewhere suggests prisons were divided into three areas of varying regime. The pit beneath **5B** was the worst, while the big room **A** with its garderobe **B** and large windows was probably for those who were detained rather than imprisoned. The floor above had its own garderobe **C** and was reached by the stairs at **D**. From the lobby above the door **E** a further flight **F** led to the roof top.

The top floor and its fireplace **A** can be ▶ identified with the courtroom, the adjacent rooms being officer accommodation. The floor of the courtroom was of timber carried on joists **B**, but there is no such arrangement between the prison floor and the basement. Instead the crosswall of the prison **C** overhangs that of the basement **D**. These anomalies are explained by the basement and its crosswall belonging to the first period tower **4B**. It was filled up prior to the building of the second, thirteenth-century structure **4A** and its crosswall **C**. The bottom floor of the first tower was lit by three round headed windows in twelfth-century style. The top of that at **E** has been destroyed, but the one at the other end of the room and cleared of its blocking is intact. The destruction associated with the damage to **E** was the occasion for the rebuilding of the tower. The old walls were reduced to the height seen at **4B** or, where badly damaged as at **E**, rebuilt to that height. The slight offset at **F** and narrow course **G** are the top of the damaged wall. The motte **2B** clearly belongs to the second period and was made by infilling the 'basement' and piling material against its walls. This was probably the work of Richard of Cornwall (c1227-72) who also refurbished the antiquated motte at nearby Launceston. Here the early tower must have been entered at first floor level, possibly by an external staircase against the north west wall, where there was no ground floor window. The general arrangements of the first structure are thus those of the second, showing it was *the* prison referred to in 1194-5.

**7**

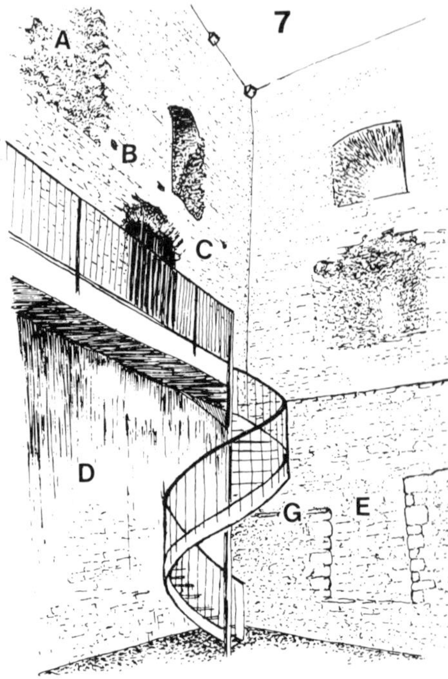


**8**

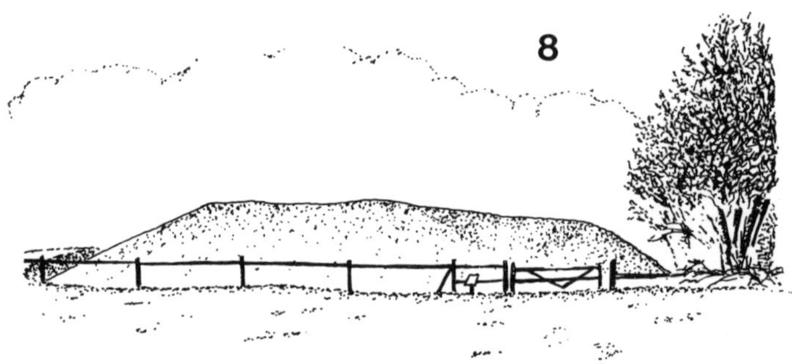

▲
Prior to the building of the prison in the late twelfth century the 'castle' was this L-shaped bank and ditch cutting off a corner of the *burgh*. The arrangement is very similar to the early castle at Exeter **8** suggesting it was constructed about the same time. Within the rampart, capped by a palisade, would be the principal (timber) buildings.

*Lydford was 'founded' by Alfred as a fortified town and the Normans established a small earthwork castle in one corner. In the late twelfth century a stone prison of at least two storeys was built nearer the centre of the town. After some disaster it was rebuilt, but in the outdated form of a motte and bailey.*

## 25 MERRIVALE
SX554747

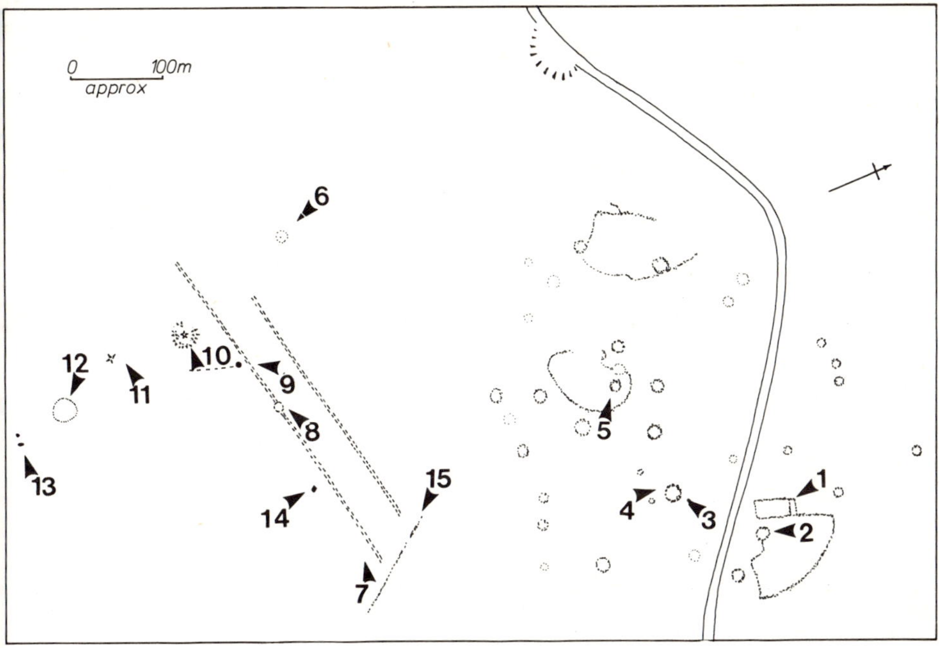


The rectangular building **A** and its adjacent croft **B** is probably the 'house' recorded as being built in the area in 1802.

2

▲
The man building that house told a visiting antiquarian that he had found 'fireplaces' and 'ashes' in many of the circular huts such as **A**.

Hut **A** appears to be contemporary with the enclosing wall **B**.

3

▲
This is one of the largest hut circles and, like many, has an entrance **A** still flanked by door jambs **B**. The adjacent wall must have been built up to their height either by drystone walling, turf, cob or wattle and daub. The base of the walls was constructed of two lines of slabs or orthostats with rubble infill as at **C**. It would not be necessary to support the roof on a central post if the roof members were linked by a wall plate or ring beam.
Significantly none of the six huts dug in 1895 had evidence for posts. Some were, however, found to be paved and hearths were identified in two.

▶

3a

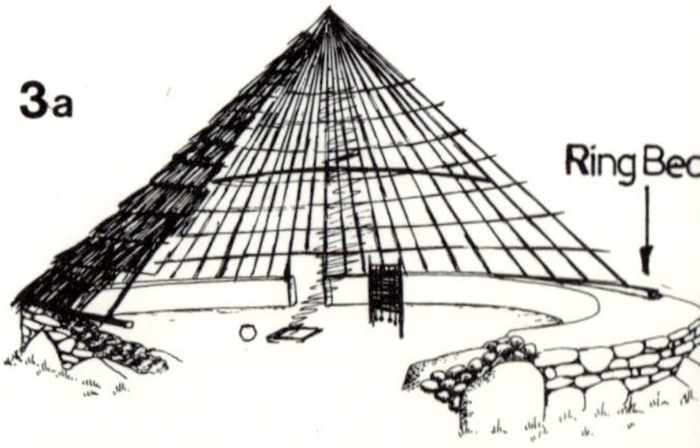

How long such buildings remained in use is unknown, but this one was substantially rebuilt — a wall of coursed stones **A** has been constructed inside that of orthostats **B**. It is possible that **A** did not directly replace **B** but was built many years, perhaps centuries, later. ▶

**4**

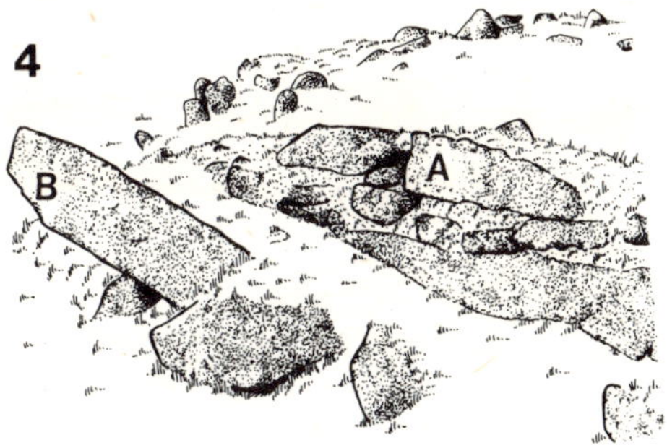


Wall **A** forms an irregular enclosure and, like **2B**, there is a hut circle **B** inside. While **B** could be contemporary with **A** it might also be earlier, having been enclosed fortuitously. The absence of fields around the enclosure suggests it was for penning stock. As stock pens are unlikely to have changed much with time the enclosure could be of any period. By analogy with other sites some of the unenclosed huts were built in the Bronze Age.
▼

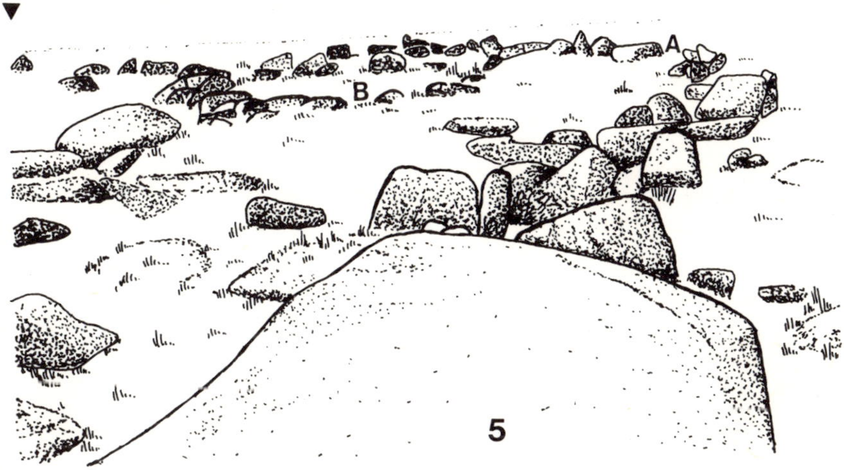


**5**

**6**

▲
It is not always possible to distinguish between Bronze Age huts for the living and contemporary ritual sites and this circle has been classed as both. The confusion reflects the close links between stone circles and huts, for some circles replaced timber huts and halls, while others had architectural features appropriate to buildings of timber structures. At Stonehenge, for example, mortice and tennon joints were used on the lintels, while the latter form a feature identical to a ring beam — see **3** above.

7

▲
Stone rows such as **A** and **B** are concentrated upon, but are not exclusive to, Dartmoor. Most are narrow like these and terminate at circles, mounds or slabs **C**. The reason, if any, for kink **D** and tall stone **E** has not been sought by excavation, but it may be that row **A** has been extended or two separate rows joined.

8

▲
Evidence from excavated examples suggests that stone rows were used and, therefore, probably built by 'Beaker' folk at the end of the Neolithic-beginning of the Bronze Age. A relatively early date here is implied by the row being overlain by another Bronze Age ritual site — a mound **A** with kerb **B**. Hollow **C** is the result of antiquarian excavation. The relationship of stone **D** to the others is not clear.

Not all rows consist of two lines or are easily visible. This row of tiny stones **A** probably led up to mound **B**, although the former is not aligned on the centre of the latter. ▶

9

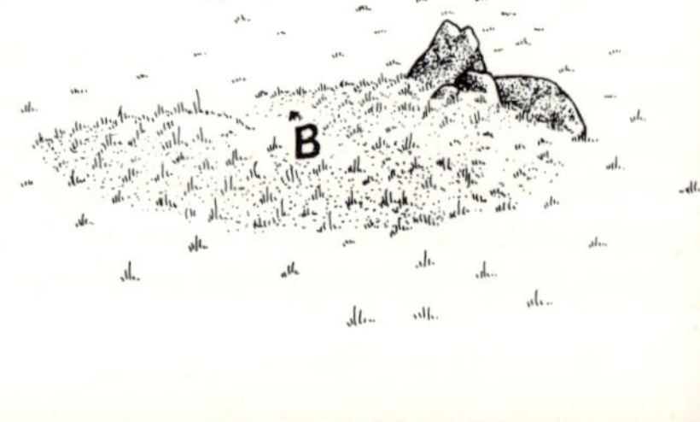

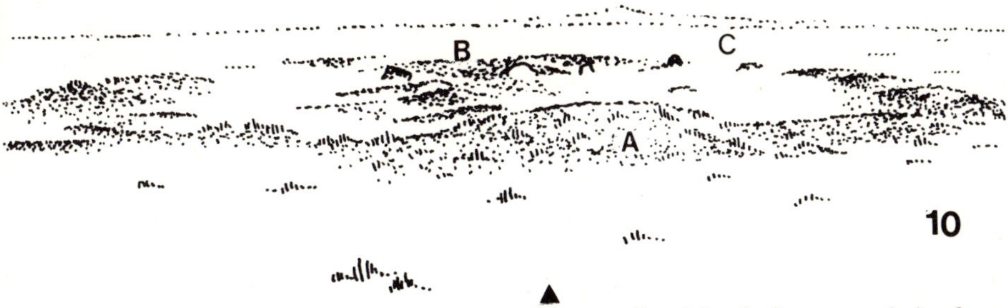


10

▲
The mutilated bank **A** surrounded a former mound **B**; an arrangement recalling the disc or saucer barrows of Wessex, except the latter have ditches. The Wessex sites belong to the Early Bronze Age. Here, there may have been an entrance through the bank at **C**.

11

▲
Small mounds like this one and **9B** could have been field clearance, for burial or both. The result of the antiquarian excavation in the centre is not known.

12

▲
Stone circle **A** has a possible 'outlier' **B**. 'Outliers' are popularly held to allow astronomical sightings, but here that would be impossible unless one was lying on the ground. Although a single trench cut in 1872 produced nothing, it is possible that the circle is an example of those in which a 'pavement' or layer of rough cobbling sealed a pit or series of pits, with or without burials. Interestingly, therefore, excavations in 1895 revealed a series of pits nearby. The pits were stone lined and the excavators believed that they once held larger stones, although why the latter should have all been removed is difficult to understand. The stone 'lining' is not inconsistent with purely 'ritual' holes.

Stone **A** originally stood upright, so the original appearance of the site was a pair of standing stones between which was a low mound or cairn **B**. Paired stones are frequently associated with or reported to be associated with cairns. Here, however there may be additional features in the form of a small alignment **C** and at least one other upright stone **D**. ▶

13

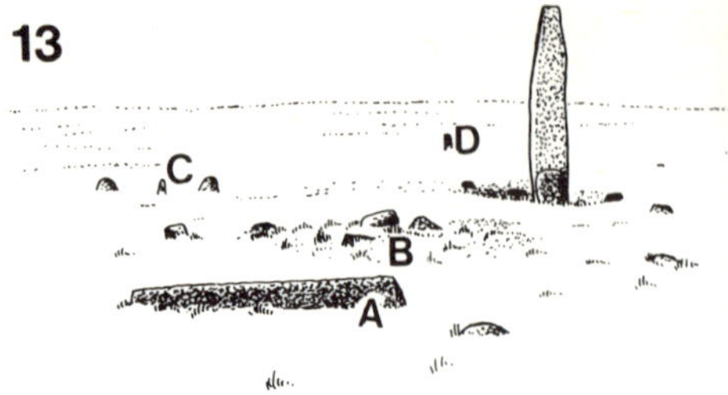


14

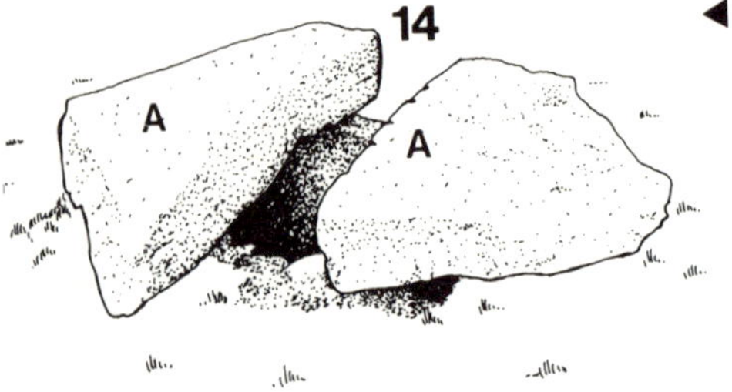


◀ This large cist was long held to be a megalithic tomb. Its capstone **A**, which was intact at the beginning of the nineteenth century was possibly always visible, although there may have been a low mound. The cist had almost certainly been plundered at an earlier period, but its size suggests it contained an inhumation burial and excavation in 1895 recovered a flint scraper, flint flake and 'polishing stone' indicating a late Neolithic-Early Bronze Age date.

15

▲
The line of stones **A** is the remains of a long Bronze Age wall or bank now known as a 'reave'. This particular example can be traced for many kilometres. It must, therefore, have been some form of boundary, if only between different kinds of land use. Gateways are found in some so they must have been more effective, ie higher, barriers than the remains suggest. Although this reave does not touch the stone rows **B** it is unlikely to be contemporary. Its relationship to the hut circles is uncertain, but they all seem to lie on the uphill side of its projected line.

*Not all the 'ritual' structures are contemporary, but evolution from and continuity with Neolithic sites is indicated. The earliest features may be the large cist, paired stones and rows. The ritual features imply extensive use and settlement of parts of the moor at the outset of the Bronze Age, but it is perhaps to a slightly later time that the visible settlement remains belong. The hut circles and reave attest extensive exploitation and management of the environment, but it is probable that not all huts are contemporary. Irregular enclosures with huts may represent a later phase of activity, but there is no direct evidence for intensive exploitation in the medieval period.*

## 26 Ringmoor Down
SX 560660

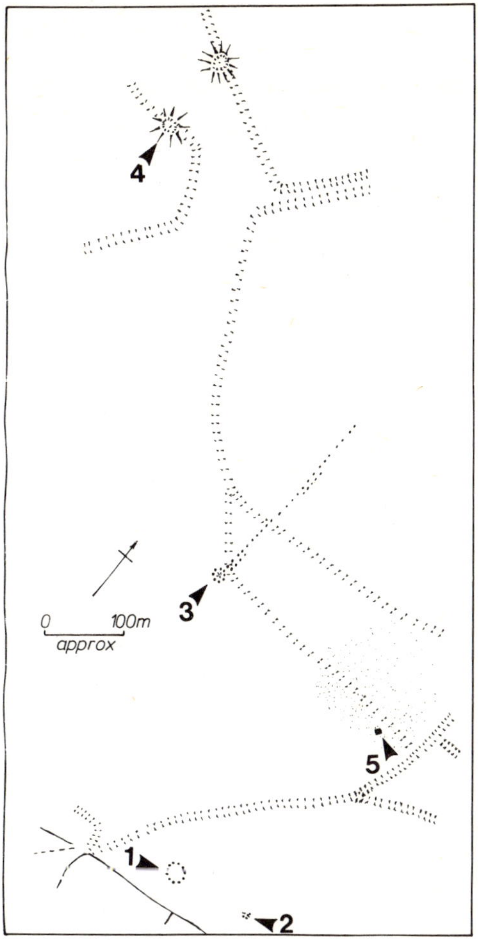


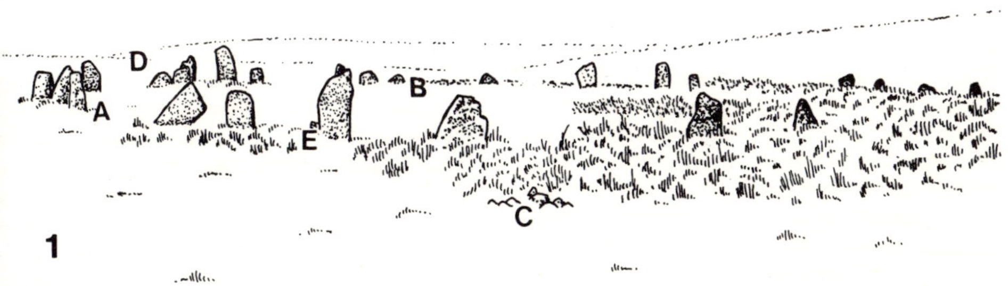


▲
The larger gaps between stones, eg **A**, may be original but are more likely to be the result of later agricultural activity. The low mound at **B** and tiny 'field clearance' heap **C** are presumably also part of that process. It is, however, possible that at least one gap, such as **D**, could be an original 'entrance'. As in analogous sites the stones have been placed in holes and wedged by small stones like those exposed at **E**. By analogy the circle is late Neolothic-Early Bronze Age in date, and is an example of those which contained no other feature unless in the form of pits.

▲
By contrast this circle is only the kerb of a low mound, presumably covering a burial. By analogy with comparable sites elsewhere it is Early Bronze Age in date.

▲
This type of circle with its central mound can also be recognised throughout the upland areas of Britain, where it again appears to be Early Bronze Age in date. On Dartmoor they might be associated with stone rows like this one and the overall plan recalls some of the 'timber circles' uncovered in lowland Britain and on the continent.

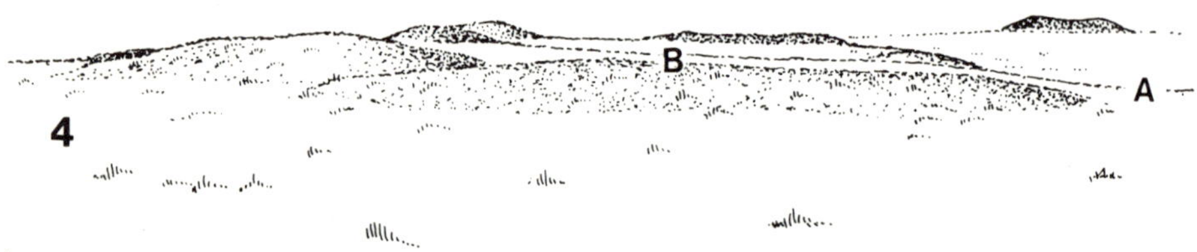


▲
Both of these mounds, subsequently damaged by field boundaries like **A**, can be paralleled elsewhere: in the Lake District for example, at Crosby Ravensworth Common **3**. The dished centre, eg **B**, is an original feature caused by the site having been built as a circular bank. In its final phase the enclosed area was sealed by tipping material inside that bank. The mounds can, therefore, be described as ring cairns. The definition of a circular area shows links with the stone circles, but the use of a bank rather than upright stones points to a variant of the tradition.

▲
It is unclear whether this cist was covered by a low mound like **2**. Its original contents are unknown, having been plundered long ago.

*Late Neolithic-Early Bronze Age ritual sites may take many forms: simple cists, mounds or mounds associated with stone circles or embanked enclosures. The same types can be recognised throughout upland Britain and the 'barrow' forms in Wessex and elsewhere in the 'lowland zone' are also related.*

## 27 Okehampton Castle
SX 584942

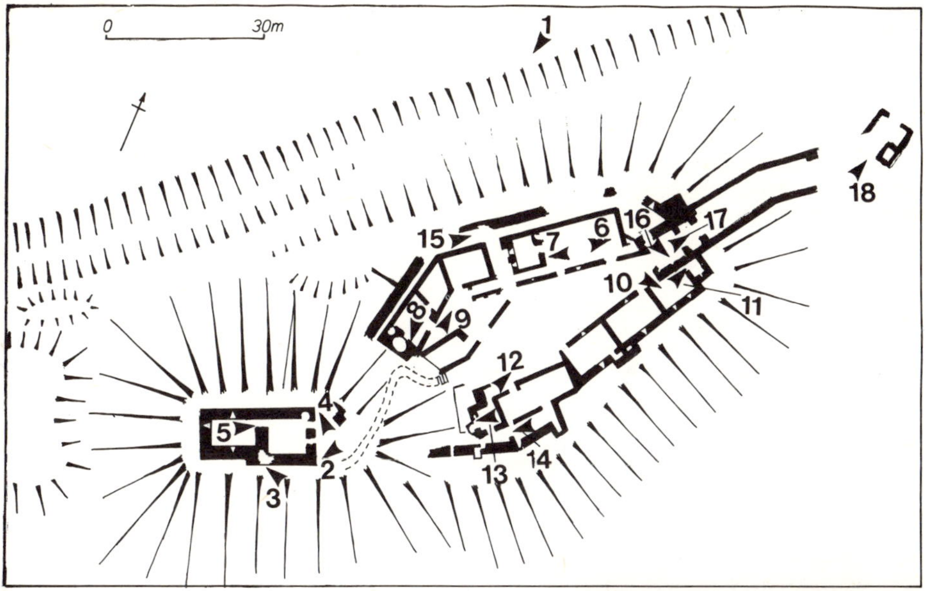

▲

Okehampton is the only castle in Devon mentioned in the Domesday Book and was, therefore, probably built in 1068-9 when the Normans advanced into Cornwall to put down a rebellion. The motte **A** and bailey **B** arrangement is a Norman one, but it may not represent the earliest castle here for the motte, or at least its top, is contemporary with the stone keep **C** and that could not have been built quickly. The castle of 1068 is more likely to have been, like Exeter and Lydford, a simple enclosure and there is such an earthwork in the woods at **D**. It consists of a simple rampart cutting off the end of the spur. The motte made use of a knob of rock, the extra material coming from the ditch around its base **E** and formerly at **F**.

The keep is of two periods, as can be seen in ▶ offset **A** and the different masonry above and below that point.

2

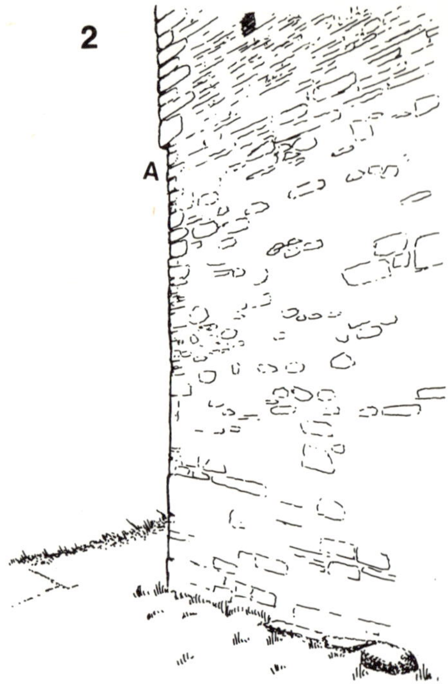

3

◀ Joint **A** marks the junction between the southern face of the early keep and its fourteenth-century extension **B**. The first structure was approximately square and it survives to the height of **C**, but how much taller it was is not known. Excavation has shown that its foundations were built at the same time as the top of the motte.

◀ Wall **A** revetted the top of the mound, but possibly only on this side where the stairs **B** were. The fourteenth-century entrance **C** had a door secured by a drawbar in hole **D**. Staircase **E** may have been the only means of access to the upper floors and to the roof where it finished in a turret.

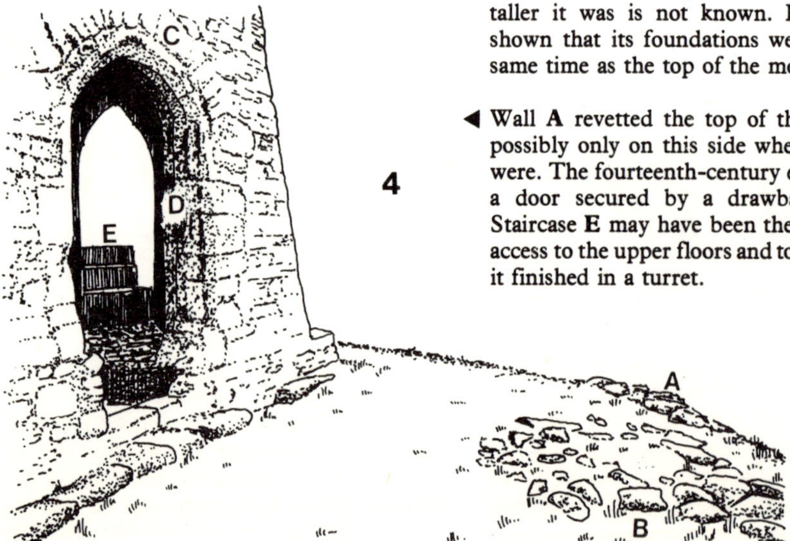


4

▲
The ground floor of the keep was for storage, with the principal accommodation above. Here there was a fireplace **A** and garderobe **B** and the window recesses would contain seats. The joists **C** of the wooden floor rested on beams **D**, while corbels **E** supported the roof timbers.

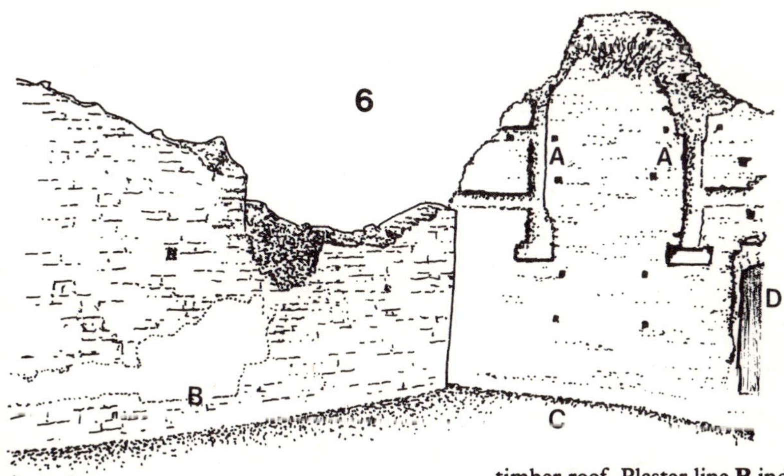


▲
The cramped keep meant the principal peace-time rooms were in the bailey. The great hall, which replaced several earlier half-timbered buildings, had a central hearth. Judging by the chasers **A** it was also provided with a complex timber roof. Plaster line **B** indicates that there was a bench down that side and the dais was probably at **C**. Behind it door **D** led to a staircase, the suite of rooms over the gate and possibly the lodgings on the other side of the courtyard.

At the other end of the hall was another private room reached by staircase **A**. It had a fireplace **B** and the same roof **C** as the hall. Beneath was the pantry **D**. ▶

**7**

**8**

▲
The pantry and hall were served by the kitchen, which had a very large oven **A** as well as a normal sized one **B**. They were heated by lighting a fire inside and then raking out the embers. Heat was retained in the stones, much like an electrical storage heater. A large number of animal bones were found on the site and analysis shows a high proportion were deer, presumably from the adjoining park.

▲
Room **A** was used for preparing fish, as numerous fish scales and bones were found in the cobbled floor. Passage **B** is an addition to the kitchen range and presumably helped protect food on its way to the hall. Its roof line **C** can still be traced.

On the opposite side of the courtyard was a series of lodgings, with fireplace **A** and garderobe **B**. The timber floor rested on joists **C**. The basement **D** was for storage.
▼

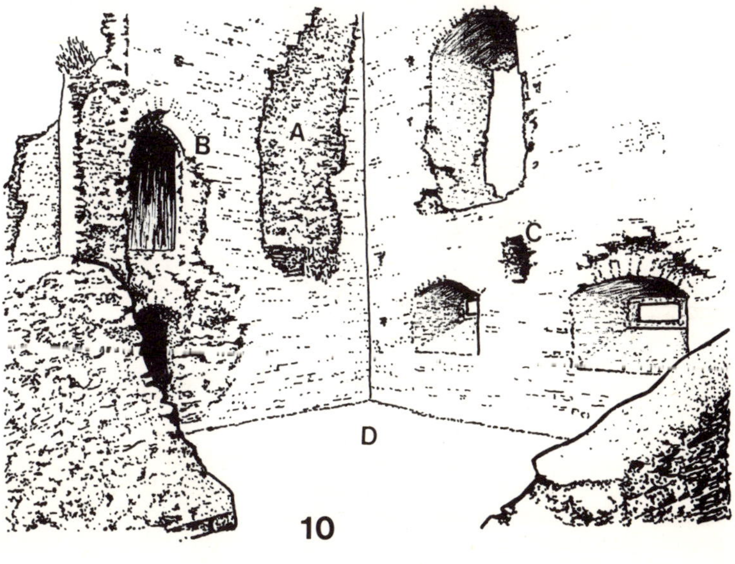

11

▲ The garderobe had a wooden seat at **A** and a wash basin with drain **B**. Water must have been brought in jugs.

12

◀ The chapel with its piscina **A** had a sloping roof **B** and a porch which can be traced in the cobbles at **C**. The rebates in **D** were for a timber door frame, an arrangement which belongs here to the seventeenth century.

13

▲
Also seventeenth century is the small kitchen with its two ovens **A** and **B** behind fireplace **C**. The bottom of **A** is a millstone, probably from the water mill which stood a little to the north east of the castle.

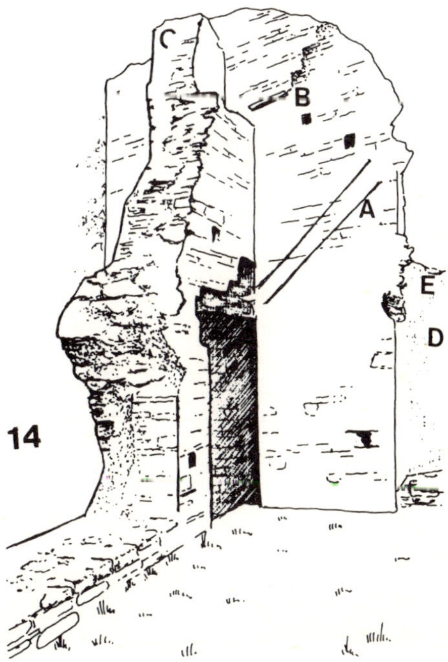


14

Roof **A** is also late, but there was an earlier 'lean to' roof **B** between the outside wall **C** and chapel area **D**. The curtain wall does not seem to have been built beyond **E**. ▶

15

▲
By contrast, on the side where the natural defences were weakest the curtain wall **A** was continued up to the inner gatehouse.

The inner gatehouse had a vaulted passage with freestone pillars **A, B** and **C**. Except at **C** all the freestone has been robbed. The shape of the vault can still be traced at **D**.
▼

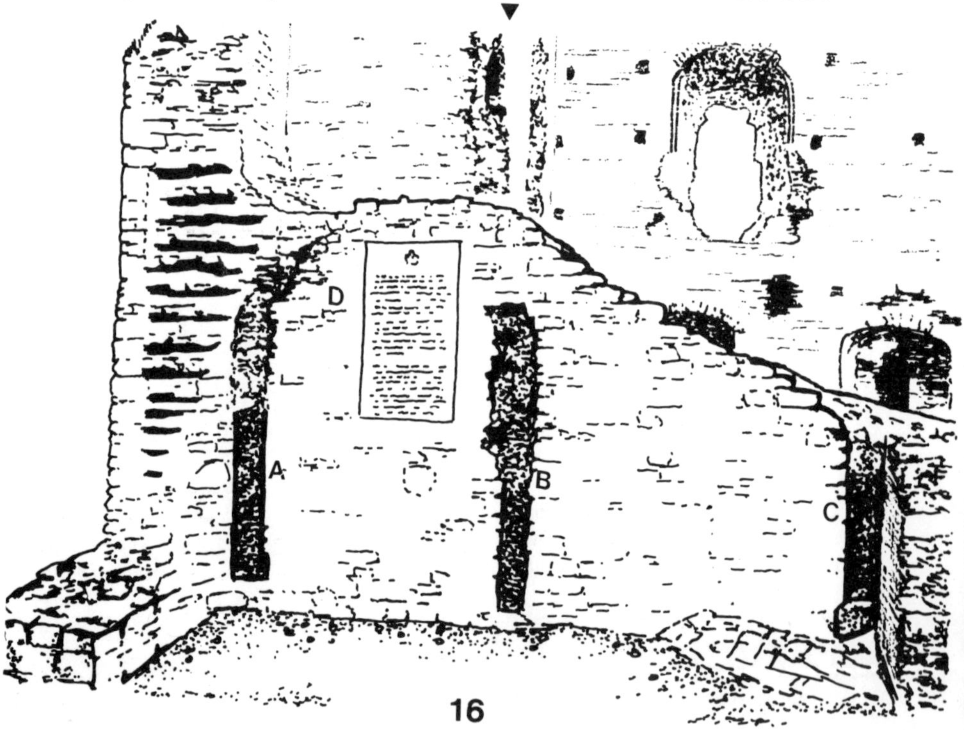


16

17

▲
The principal gatehouse was connected to the outer one **A** by a walled passage **B**, which must have functioned like a barbican.

18

▲
The outer portal had no provision for a portcullis: the gates simply closed against **A**. Over the passageway was a room with window **B** and garderobe **C**.

*Most of the stonework belongs to the fourteenth century. The plan is, however, influenced by its predecessor: a motte and bailey with stone tower. The rest of the early defences and buildings were of timber or half-timber construction. The motte and bailey may, or may not, have been the first castle here.*

SX 659860-664867

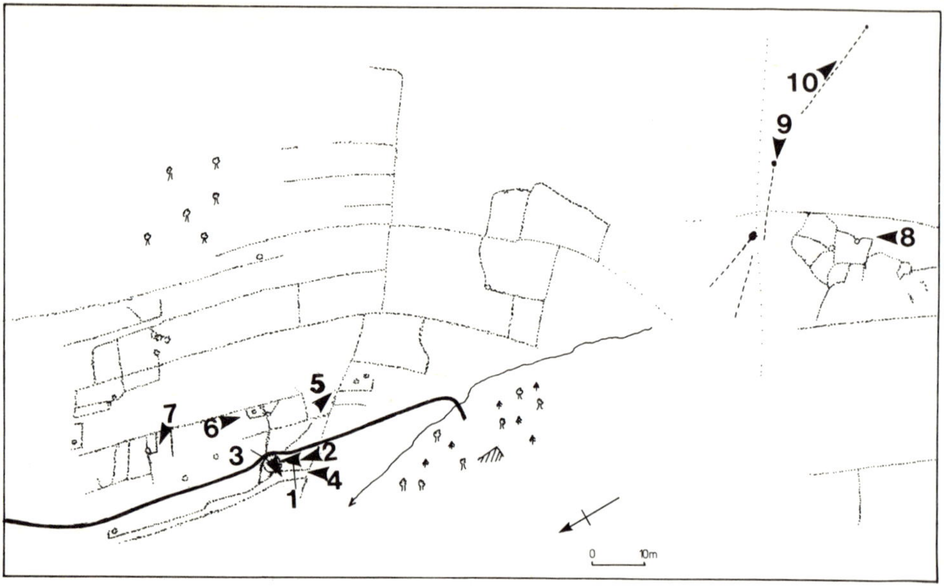


1

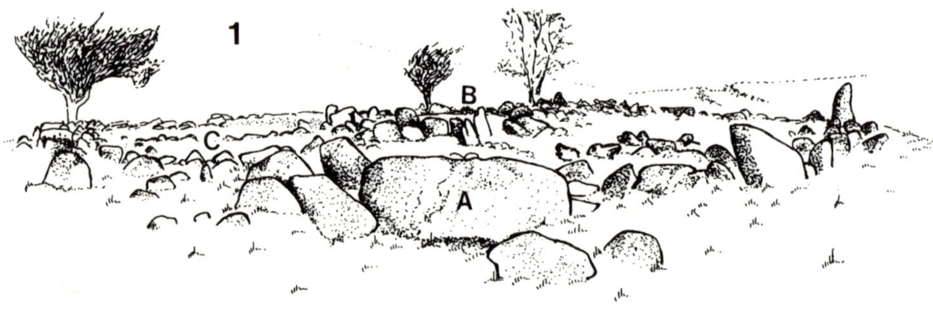


▲
The enclosure formed by wall **A** contains a circular house **B** and must be presumed to be a farmstead. The space between **A** and **B** has been subdivided into a series of yards, eg **C**.

▲
A gateway between two of the yards survives at **A**. Excavation of the hut floor — which was built as a terrace **B** — revealed a D-shaped arrangement of posts, an iron smelting furnace and a forging pit. While the excavator thought all the features were contemporary they need not have been. The furnace could have been constructed in a ruined or refurbished house and the posts could represent an earlier hut, for timber structures are known to precede stone ones at a number of sites.

▲
The perimeter of the prehistoric farmstead had a single gateway **A** which opened onto a track running to left and right.

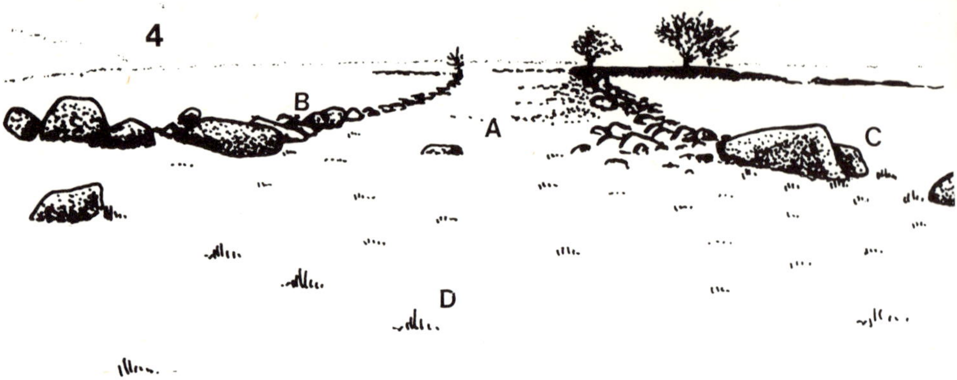


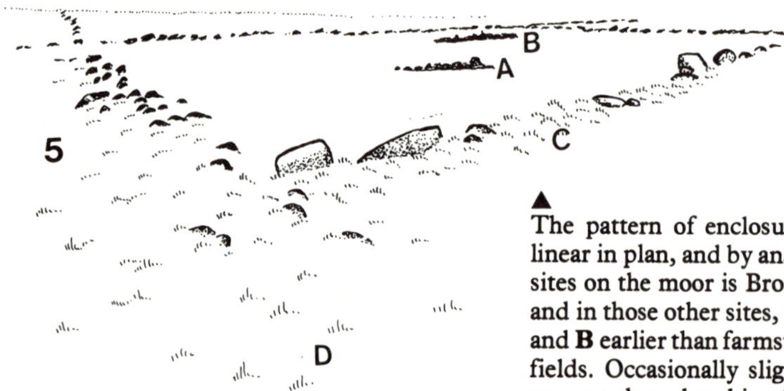


▲
The pattern of enclosures is markedly recti-linear in plan, and by analogy with comparable sites on the moor is Bronze Age in date. Here, and in those other sites, single round houses **A** and **B** earlier than farmstead **1** occur within the fields. Occasionally slight terraces such as **C** suggest that ploughing has been practised. **D** may have been an original gateway between enclosures.

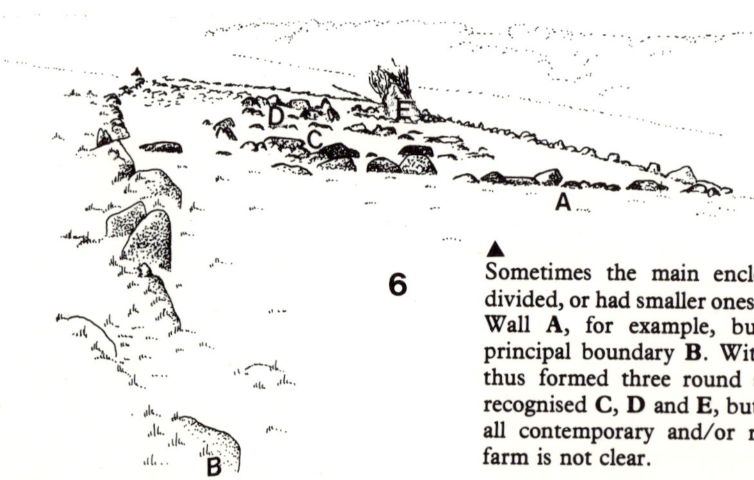


▲
Sometimes the main enclosures were sub-divided, or had smaller ones tacked onto them. Wall **A**, for example, butts up against a principal boundary **B**. Within the enclosure thus formed three round structures can be recognised **C**, **D** and **E**, but whether they are all contemporary and/or represent a single farm is not clear.

◀ Southwards the trackway **A** ran between enclosures such as **B** and **C** until it reached open land **D**. The width of **A** indictes that it was a droveway, so the system would appear to have included an area of open or rough grazing **D** and an area of enclosed land, **B** and **C**, supporting crops, hay or better pasture.

▲ Excavation of the interior of hut **A** revealed an internal ring of posts, with a single one in the centre. The number of posts must have made the interior somewhat crowded and it is difficult to see why they were all needed, unless the roof was exceptionally heavy. It is possible that not all the features were contemporary although they were all spaced equally. Again, the chronological relationship of the hut to the adjoining walls, eg **B**, is not clear.

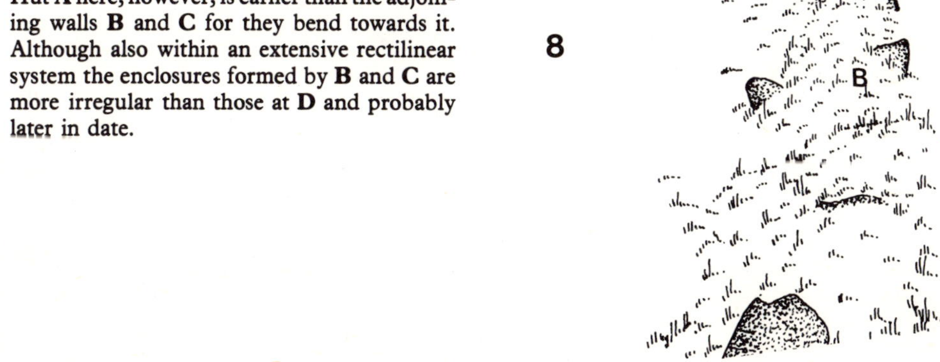


▲ Hut **A** here, however, is earlier than the adjoining walls **B** and **C** for they bend towards it. Although also within an extensive rectilinear system the enclosures formed by **B** and **C** are more irregular than those at **D** and probably later in date.

9

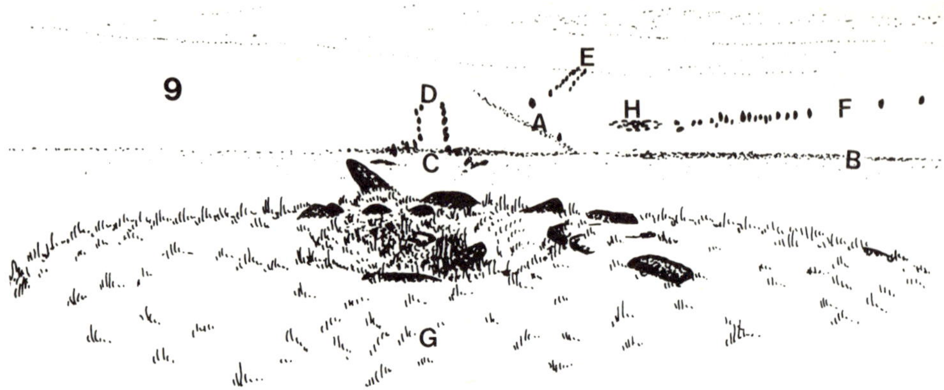


▲
The small, Bronze Age rectilinear enclosures, such as those at **8D**, are subdivisions of larger tracts formed by linear boundaries or reaves **A** and **B**. The reaves, however, ignore or overlie, eg at **C**, the stone rows **D**, **E** and **F** showing the latter to be earlier, ie late Neolithic-Early Bronze Age. Such rows can terminate at mounds like **G**, or in circles **H**. The circles at **H** appear to be within a low mound and recall the circles of stakes found beneath some contemporary barrows. Although the reaves overlie the stone rows, the ground in this area has not been subdivided to the same extent as at **8** and **8D**. This may be due to the proximity of the stream as much as to the sanctity of the rows, for the reave enclosures at **4** stop short of the stream.

The purpose of the stone rows is not clear. They would seem to have been designed for ceremony or processions even though some are, like this one, very narrow. The row terminated at monolith **A**.
▼

10

*Late Neolithic-Early Bronze Age rows imply the presence of a substantial local population on the moor at that time but later in the Bronze Age much of the landscape was divided into units which respected and were perhaps based upon stream/valley systems. The rectilinear blocks so formed were sometimes sub-divided and isolated round houses constructed. Later, probably in the Iron Age, a number of enclosed farms were built and the earlier fields utilised, modified or abandoned in parts. When intensive agriculture fell back to its present limit is not clear.*

## 29 Grimspound
SX 700809

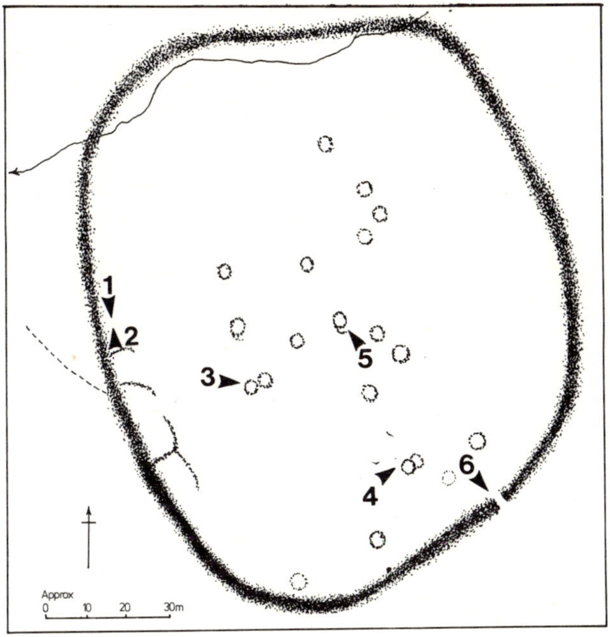

▲The pound, at an altitude of 1500 ft (457 m), contains a number of hut circles such as **A**. The sub-rectangular enclosures **B** are of unknown date, but may be contemporary with **A** or the perimeter wall **C** or both. **B** were probably stock pens or small cultivated plots but in either case they must have been more substantial than now.

2

▲
A factor in the siting of the pound and similar enclosures seems to have been the proximity of water, and here stream **A** flows through the interior. The importance of water suggests the management of large numbers of stock and that may explain the massive perimeter wall. Built with inner and outer skins **B** and **C** and rubble core **D** it may originally have carried a fence or hedge.

The walls of the huts were built like the perimeter one and must have been at least as high as the tallest stone or jamb **A**. As no evidence for a central post was found in early excavations the roof must have been self supporting, the rafters being joined at the wall top. The arrangement of two huts **B** and **C** back-to-back can be paralleled at Dean Moor, but it may be that **B** and **C** are not contemporary.
▼

3

4

▲
Construction at different periods can perhaps be inferred here where curving wall **A** is intersected by hut **B**.

*The settlement was predominantly pastoral and, as the later name implies, connected with stock. Not all the structures were contemporary and use may have been seasonal. Even allowing for a better climate in the Bronze Age winter, occupation at this altitude would have been miserable.*

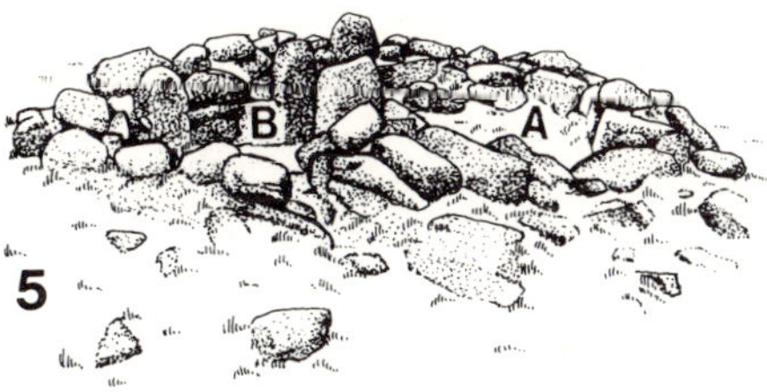


5

◀ It is unusual to have a hut **A** with a smaller room or porch **B**, but there are again parallels at Dean Moor where the little room, apparently not a porch, contained a pit. Dean Moor has been dated to the Middle Bronze Age.

The entrance to the pound faces uphill, indicating that the principal pastures were in that direction. The absence of any fields or boundaries adjoining the perimeter is in contrast to the situation at Kestor, and a different kind of land management must be inferred. Here a predominantly pastoral economy must have been practised. Whether occupation was continuous or seasonal is, however, difficult to determine. ▶

6

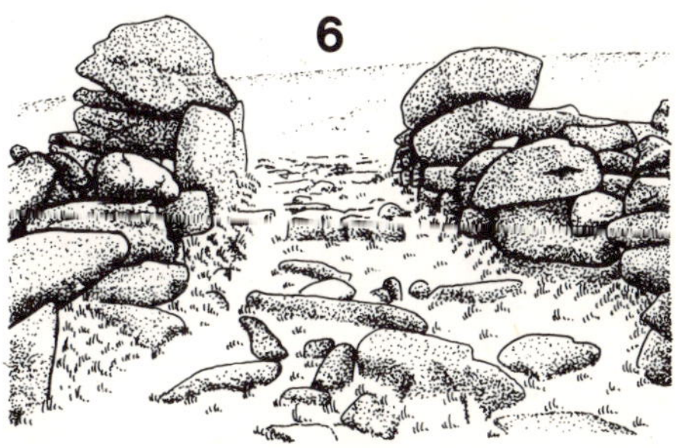

## 30 Hound Tor
SX 748790

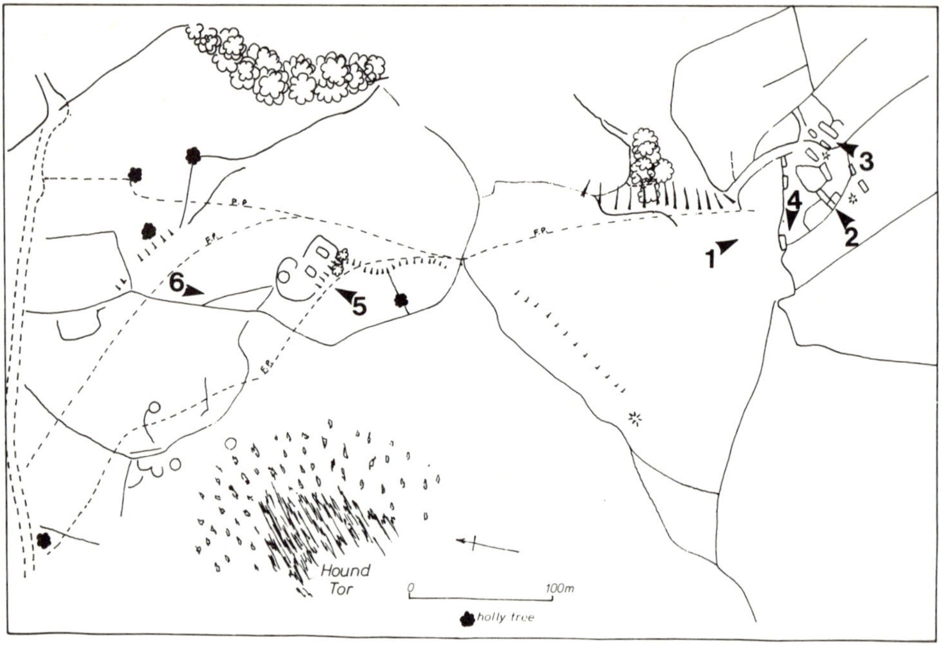


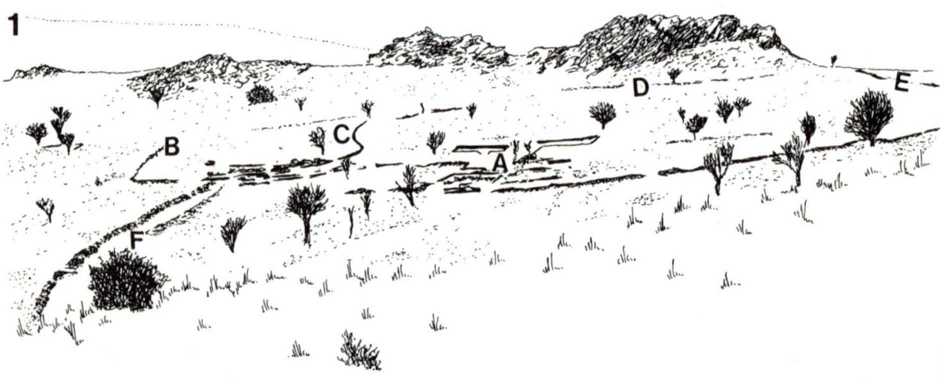


▲
The village **A** stood amongst a number of large enclosures formed by boundaries such as **B, C, D** and **E,** and was served by lanes like **F**. By the fourteenth century climatic deterioration made it impractical to farm a unit the size of a peasant's and the settlement was abandoned.

House **A** has tentatively been identified as the ▶ manor house, primarily because it seems to lie within its own crofts and has extra buildings **B** and **C**.

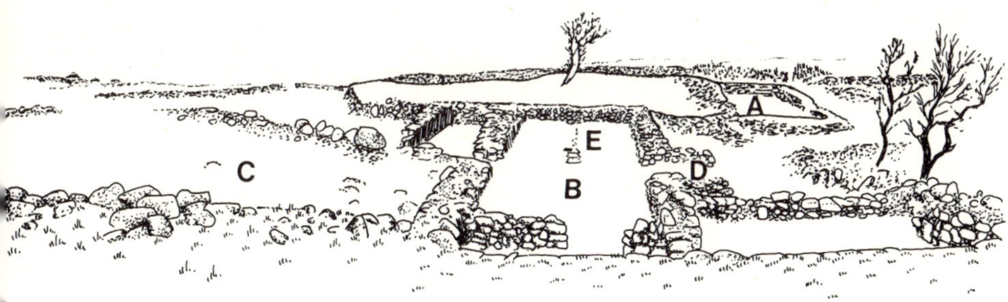


2

▲

The houses, like **A** and **B**, appear to be loosely grouped either side of a lane and with a croft **C** behind each. Each house also had a door and porch **D** in the centre of a long side. Drains such as **E** show that the byre was under the same roof as the family. If the walls were much higher than at present they were probably constructed of a less durable material than stone, eg turf or cob. The excavators found that stone walls had not been built before the thirteenth century, prior to that they were largely of turf. While turf walls are good insulators their life is short — about 30 years — and the evidence here suggests some buildings had to be rebuilt eight times. Beneath the turf predecessors of **B** were three earlier buildings partly sunk into the hillside and interpreted as the remains of shieling huts — temporary cabins for herdsmen or shepherds on summer grazing grounds. Such pasturing clearly represents a less intensive land use than that practised by the village, but cannot be dated. The site has produced no pottery from before the twelfth century, but the area was intensively farmed by the time of the Domesday Survey: 'The abbot [of Tavistock] has a manor called Hundetorra . . . and it rendered yield for half a hide. This can be ploughed by 4 ploughs. Rainald holds this of the abbot. Of it R has 1 virgate and 1 plough in desmesne and the villeins 1 virgate and 1 plough. Here R has 2 villeins, 4 bordars, 2 serfs, 7 oxen, 28 sheep, 18 goats, 2 acres of wood, 9 acres of meadow and 1 league of pasture.'

3

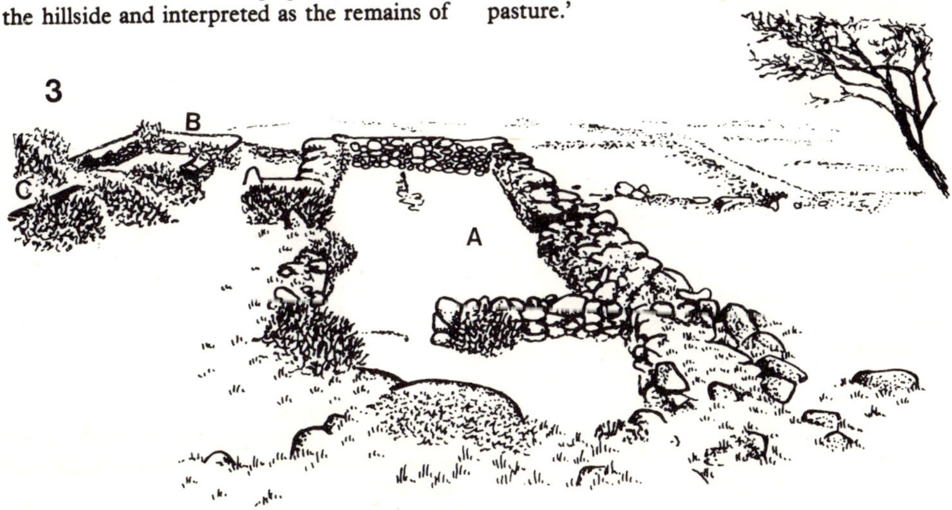

4

It is possible that some of the population listed in the Domesday Survey lived in isolated farms like this one, where two rectangular buildings **A** and **B** and a kiln at **C** were enclosed by a wall **D**. The enclosing wall was, however, part of a prehistoric farmstead which contained a round hut beneath **A** and another at **E**. **E** was refurbished and used by the medieval farmer.
▼

▲
Corn drying kilns like **A** show that cereals were being grown in the thirteenth century as well as at the time of Domesday.

5

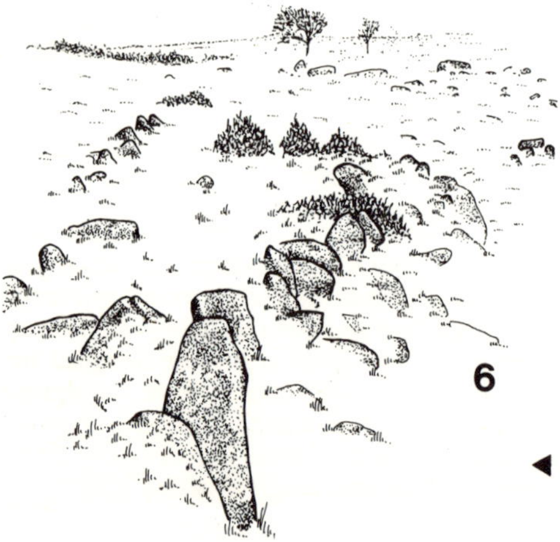

6

*The margin of intensive land use has fluctuated. The area farmed in prehistoric times was subsequently used for summer grazing, until the re-establishment of intensive land use in the medieval period. Some of the new settlements utilised existing sites, former shielings or abandoned prehistoric farms.*

◀ It is unclear whether the walls and enclosures adjacent to the farmstead are prehistoric or medieval.

## 31 BERRY POMEROY CASTLE
SX839623

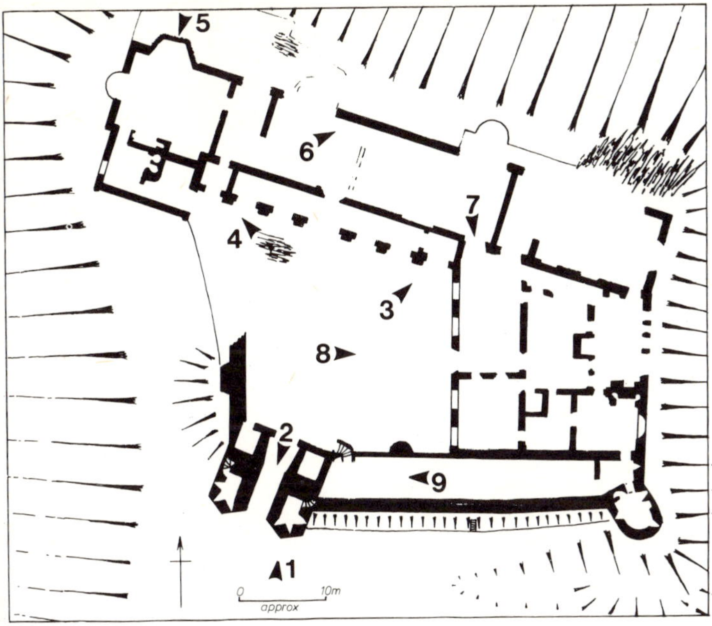


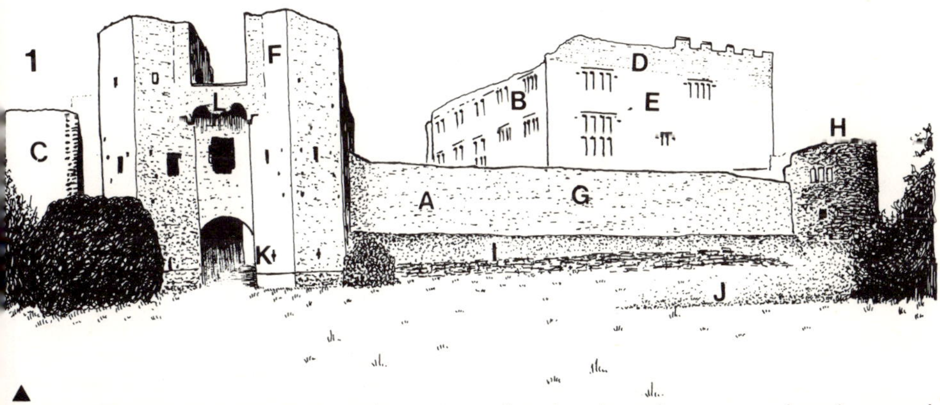


▲

The remains are of two main periods, the fifteenth-century castle of the Pomeroys **A** and the half-finished palace **B** and **C** of Edward Seymour, Duke of Somerset and Protector of Edward VI. Seymour bought the site in 1548, but was executed in 1552. The castle was approximately square in plan with a principal residential block **B**, altered and raised in height by Seymour as can be seen from the difference in masonry between **D** and **E**. The gatetower **F** was at one corner of the curtain wall **G**, while at the other three there seem to have been semi-circular towers such as **H**. The bank and retaining wall **I** are modern, but ditch **J** is ancient. Whether the ditch extended in front of **F** is not known, but the latter was heavily defended. The loops at **K** were designed for hand cannon, while the roofs of the towers were massively reinforced for engines or guns. Machicolation **L** allowed missiles to be dropped on those attacking the portal.

2

▲ The gates closed against **A** and were secured by a drawbar **B**, while being protected by portcullis **C**. Blocked doorway **D** presumably led into a guard chamber or porter's lodge.

The medieval buildings were ranged around a courtyard and must have been extensive, for in the late fifteenth century only one part consisted of 'a great chamber beyond the castle gate with the cellar on the left of the gate with two chambers beyond and belonging to the great chamber, a kitchen, a larder house, a chamber beyond the kitchen, a pantry, a buttery and the *Steuardis* chamber'. To these must be added the great hall, kitchen and main residential block. The visible remains are those ▼ of the palace with its large windows **A**. The even larger windows, eg **B** and **C**, have collapsed leaving the pillars, eg **D**, between. **B** and **C** helped light the new principal range in front of which was a loggia, **E**, **F** and **G** being the bases for the open arcade. Recess **H** held the entablature above the arcade and above it was a balustrade. At either end was a doorway **I** leading to a staircase.

3

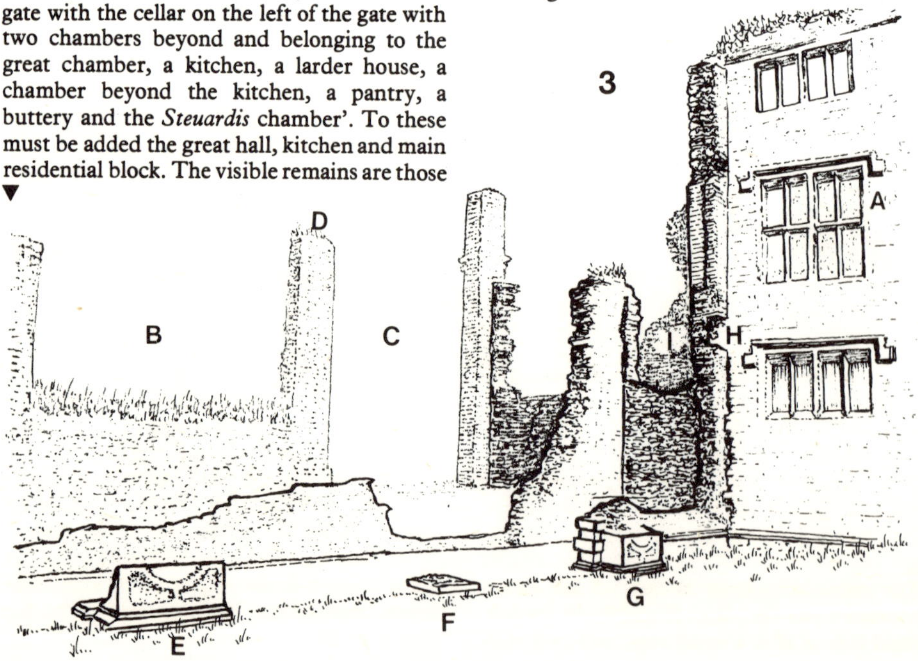

At the back of the loggia was a series of niches **A**. Blocked doorway **B**, however, represents a later modification for although the loggia and northern range seem to have been completed the overall design for the palace was not. Rock outcrop **C**, for example, was not removed to make a level courtyard and the western range was never built, although provision for bonding it to the rest of the building **D** was made. The abandonment of the overall design must be attributed to Seymour's execution and the subsequent loss of finance. The house was occupied until the late seventeenth century when it was deserted and rapidly became a ruin.

▼

**4**

**5**

▲

The necessarily large kitchen of the palace contained two fireplaces **A** and **B**. In the left-hand side of **B** is a small oven and two more exist in the bakehouse (?) **C**. The kitchen and river front of the building was lit by bay-windows **D**.

▲
The great hall was at first floor level and lit by the bay window at **A**. That at **B** lit a chamber divided from the hall by wall **C**. Below the chamber was a service room with arched doorway or vault **D**. The difference in masonry between **E** and **F** suggests that the latter is part of the medieval building.

The principal door into the hall **A** was reached by a great staircase at **B**. The stairs may have been built within the shell of the drastically remodelled medieval hall for the doors at **C** recall those between a medieval hall and its kitchen.
▼

A retention of part of the medieval fabric may account for joints **A** and **B** which do not continue above **C**. **C** is the height of the earlier building — see **1D** and **1E**. This side of the earlier structure was wholly refaced, but narrow course **C** implies it was after the addition of **1D**, for the course can have served no practical purpose other than levelling up to allow the blocks above to be tied to those of the side. A promenade retained by a new wall **D** and the old curtain **1G** was then added.

▼

**8**

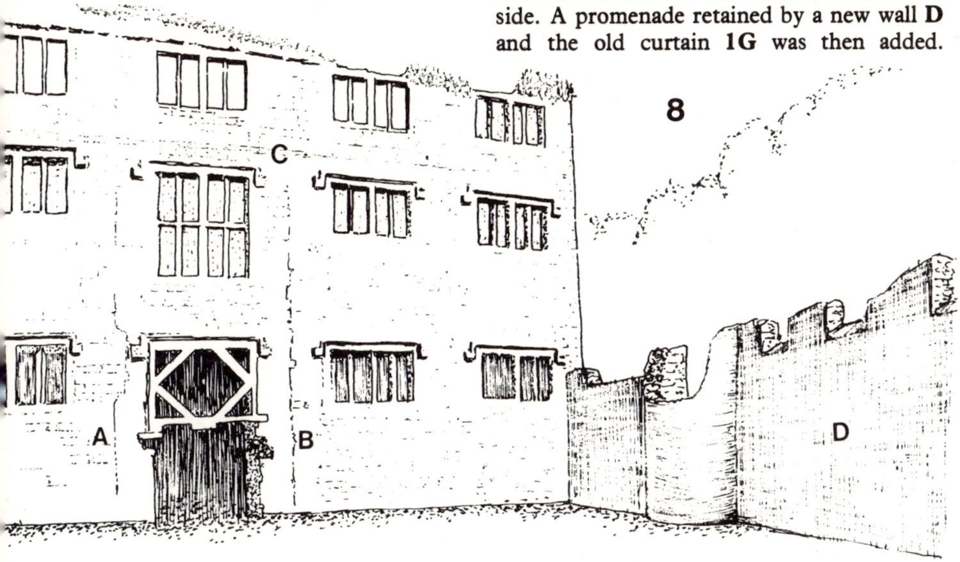

**9**

▲

Door **A** led from the gatehouse to the parapet of the curtain wall which also seems to have been reached by a staircase at **B**. Door **C** may belong to the sixteenth-century promenade **D**, but the room into which it opened was important before that time, for it contains a late fifteenth-century fresco depicting the Adoration of the Magi. The room may, therefore, have been the castle's chapel even though it also served the portcullis.

*The medieval castle of the Pomeroy's was quadrangular in plan, with an inner range partly incorporated in Seymour's sixteenth-century palace. The latter was never finished.*

## 32 MILBER DOWN
SX884698

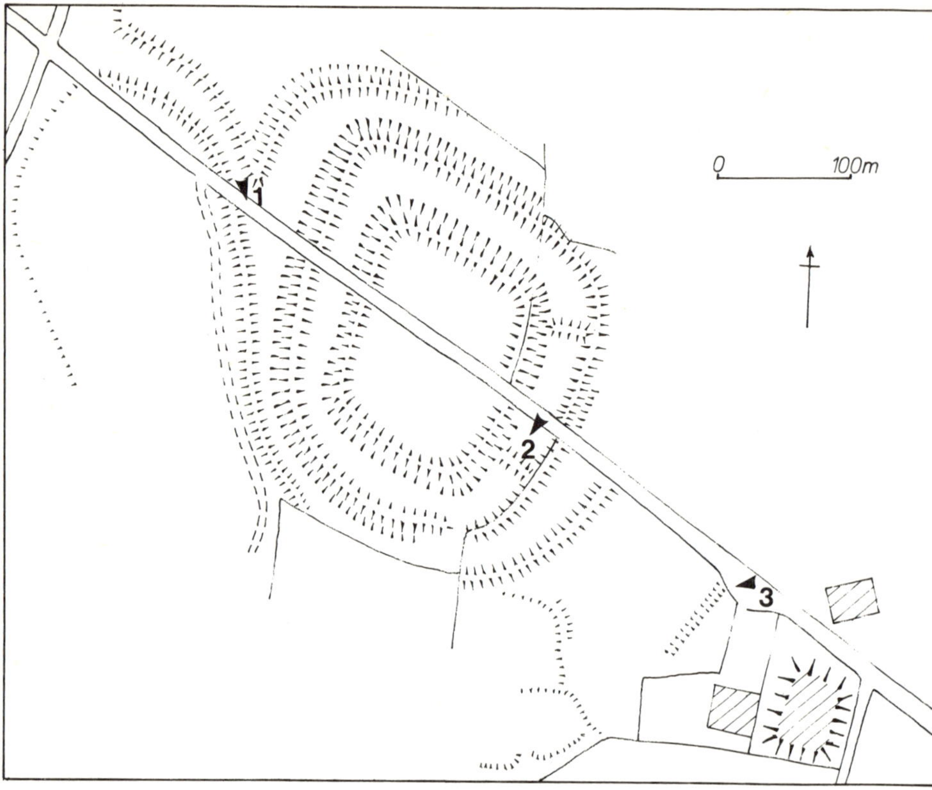

2

▲
Such an interpretation is consistent with cross banks like **A** dividing up the space between the ramparts.

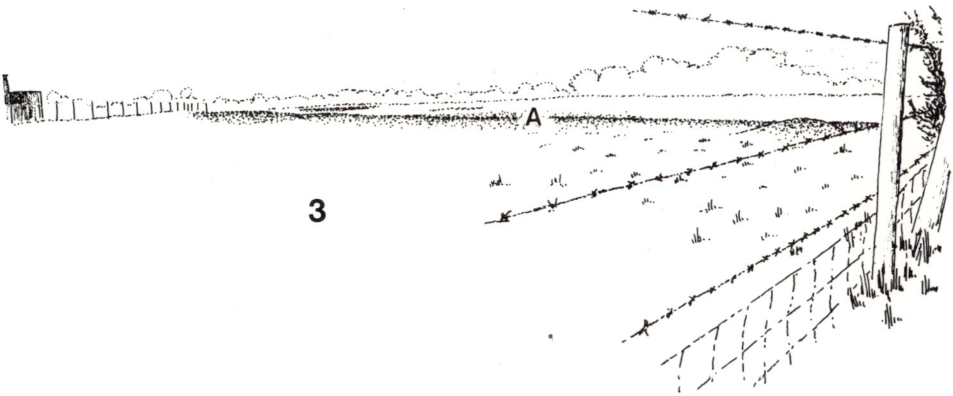


3

◀ The 'fort' has three ramparts **A, B** and **C** each with a ditch. The site is, however, defensively weak for it is on a slope and not on the hilltop and the ramparts are widely spaced: characteristics possessed by a number of late Iron Age sites in South West England. Excavations here showed a similar date and that the site was abandoned by the middle of the first century AD, when three miniature bronzes were buried or hidden in the middle ditch. Like the other examples of the type this site seems to be positioned in relation to a water supply, for rampart **A** swings outwards to become a lane leading downhill. It has, therefore, been suggested that this type of site was concerned with a predominantly pastoral economy; the widely spaced ramparts being used to contain and protect the stock.

▲
It is, however, possible that bank **2A** was part of a slightly later field system and farm to which earthworks **A** belong. Excavation showed that the farm was occupied in the Roman period and that its fields were entered by gaps cut in the outer rampart of the 'fort'. Whether the farm was the direct successor of the 'fort' is uncertain, but the numerous fields imply that farming became more intensive. The change may reflect the impact of Rome, there being a demand for surplus produce in local and distant markets.

*The 'hillslope forts' with widely spaced ramparts are late prehistoric in date and pastoral in origin. In the Roman period agriculture was more intensive.*

**33 Torre Abbey**
SX 908638

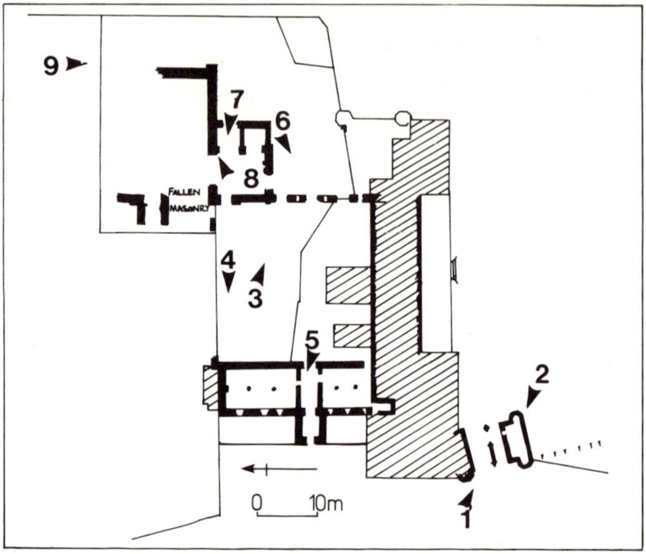


At its dissolution in 1539 the abbey was the richest Praemonstratensian house in the country. Something of that wealth can be seen in the great barn **A** and fourteenth-century gatehouse **B**. The barn is a reminder that monasteries were the centres of extensive land holdings, either farmed by the brethren themselves or for them, and that apart from the church and conventual buildings the abbey consisted of an outer court with the buildings and equipment of a normal farm. Traditionally the barn held tithes and later Spanish (Armada) prisoners. The outer court was enclosed by a wall at **C** and gateway **B** was one of the few points of entry, the arches being closed by gates.

▼

It was usual to lodge guests in the rooms of the gatehouse or nearby and the building whose roof line can be seen at **A** must have served that purpose or as stables or both. Door **B** indicates that it had an upper floor.

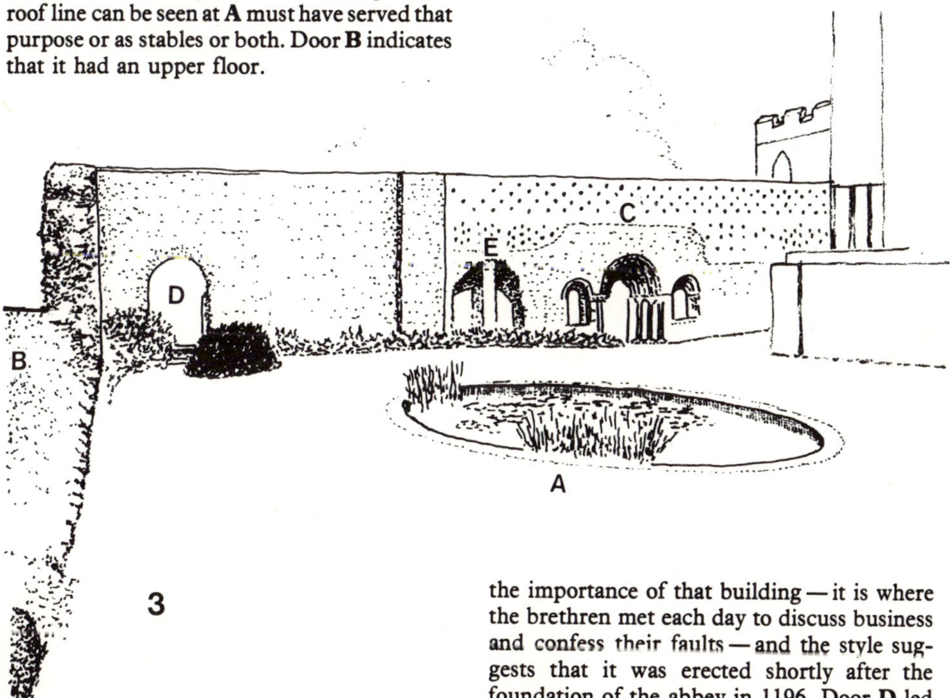


▲
The buildings of the inner court or convent were grouped around the cloisters **A**. To the north was the church **B** and to the east the chapter house **C**. The ornate entrance reflects the importance of that building — it is where the brethren met each day to discuss business and confess their faults — and the style suggests that it was erected shortly after the foundation of the abbey in 1196. Door **D** led into the south transept of the church and allowed the canons to move freely between their work in the cloisters and the choir stalls. A passage or slype **E** led to the outer court and cemetery.

▲
The cloisters were used for meditation, reading and writing. Around the four sides was an alley with a lean to roof — line **A** — supported on corbels such as **B**.

Windows **C** and **D** are clearly later, but **E** may be original. The upper floor of the western range **F** probably contained the abbott's accommodation and the hall where he could entertain important guests.

▶

▲
The undercroft, eg **A**, was used for storage. The passageway **B** linked the cloisters with the outside world.

The alternately coloured stone over the doorway of the chapter house **A** is similar to that of Exeter bridge also built in the late twelfth century. Rough stonework **B** and **C** shows that the chapter house was vaulted. Above and occupying the first floor of the eastern range was the canons' dormitory.
▼

7

▲
As the canons had to sing night offices a staircase led from the dormitory directly into the south transept **A** of the church. The outline of the staircase can be traced in the patched stonework **B**. Above the staircase was a window **C** and the roof was vaulted. Part of that vault survives **D** amongst the collapsed remains of the central tower. The tower was carried by pillars such as **E** which rose into arch **F**.

The pillar, arch and vault are in the Norman rather than Early English styles. ▶

7a

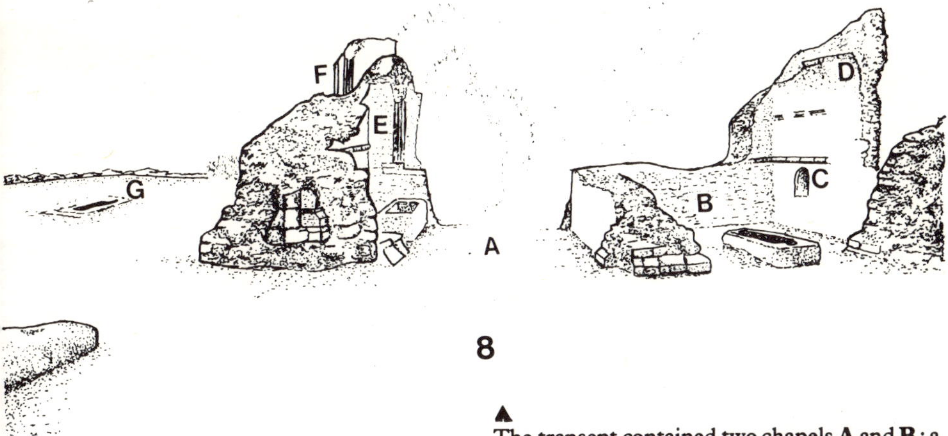


8

▲
The transept contained two chapels **A** and **B**: a piscina **C** and part of the vault **D** surviving. The latter seems to have been in the simple early style but window **E** and that behind the high altar **F** have the elaborate moulding of a later date. The grave in front of the high altar **G** belonged to the younger son of the abbey's founder.

9

▲
It was unusual to have another building **A** so near the eastern end of the church and chapter house. The purpose of **A** is unknown but it may have been the infirmary or a gate between the cemetery and outer court.

*The abbey was built to the usual monastic plan and consisted of conventual buildings arranged around cloisters with an outer court entered through gatehouses. The gatehouses could accommodate guests and both in and outside the courts were farm buildings.*

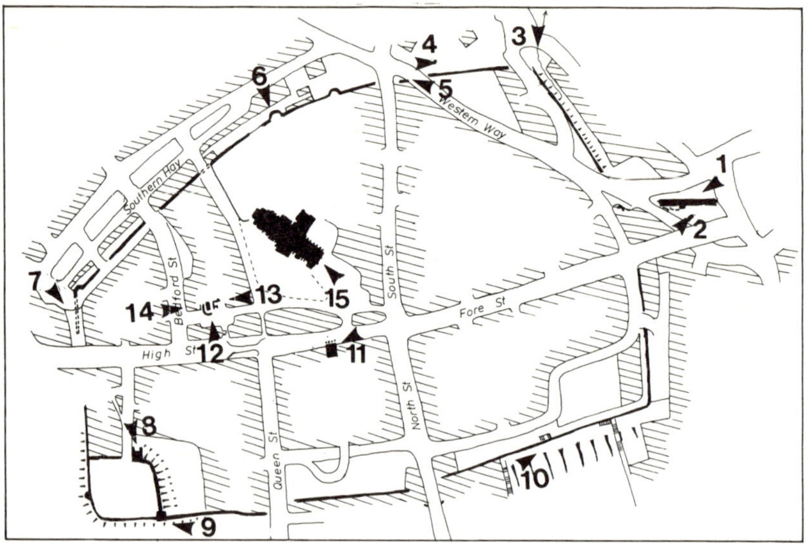


1

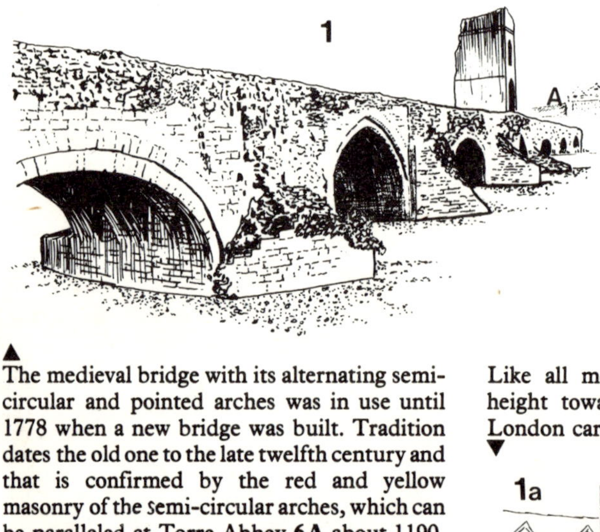


▲
The medieval bridge with its alternating semi-circular and pointed arches was in use until 1778 when a new bridge was built. Tradition dates the old one to the late twelfth century and that is confirmed by the red and yellow masonry of the semi-circular arches, which can be paralleled at Torre Abbey **6A** about 1190. Originally there seem to have been seventeen arches so almost half the bridge has survived. The great length indicates the width over which the river spread itself — the flood plain. Even so the western end was affected by flooding and early in the fifteenth century the church there, St Thomas', had to be demolished and rebuilt on its present site. At the other end the bridge led to the west gate of the city, only one side of which now remains **A**.

Like all medieval bridges this one rose in height towards the centre and like that of London carried houses:
▼

1a

▲
Holes for timbers supporting houses can be seen in pier **A**. In addition to the houses there were three churches or chapels including the old St Thomas'. The tower of St Edmund's **B** is, however, nineteenth century as is its north wall **C** and corner **D**. Its medieval predecessor was narrower and allowed the river to pass beneath. The medieval north wall was supported by separate piers, eg **E**, but columns **F** are not part of the original arrangement. The building at **G** had its own arch **H** spanning the backwater channel **I**. Building **J** lies parallel to that channel in a manner reminiscent of mills.

▲
The water course beneath **2H** must have been very like **A** here and indeed **A** may be its descendant, flowing beneath the river cliff at the edge of the former flood plain. Along that cliff was built the city wall **B**. Its blocked Watergate **C** led to the port. From Roman times until the reign of Edward I ships were able to come up river as far as the bridge, but then the weir built by Isabella, Countess of Devon, stopped the trade. In 1540, however, a short canal using an old mill leat was turned into one of the first true canals and the weir by-passed. As trade grew and the ships got bigger the canal was enlarged and lengthened and a new customs house **D** built.

The city wall has been greatly patched, but the original medieval face — if it ever had a single face — consisted of neat blocks **A** with a plinth **B**. The centre was rubble, but the cobbles at **C** are modern, sealing the core exposed when the new road **D** was sliced through. ▶

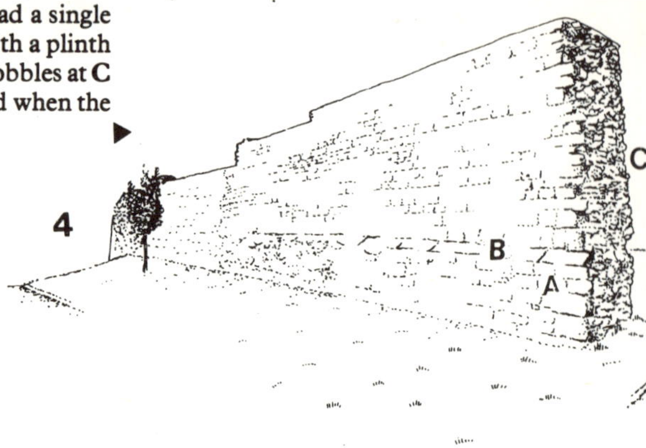


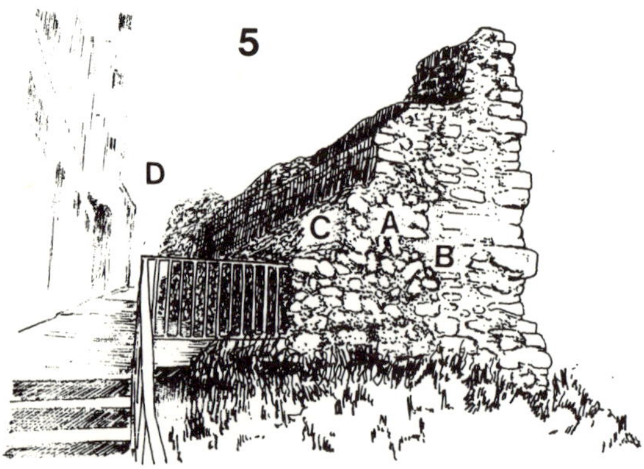


The original core **A** was from time to time cut back as new structures were built behind. Yet the medieval front **B** also seems to have been added, for its stonework differs from **A**. Excavations elsewhere have shown that the core is substantially Roman and the face to have been mostly replaced since then. Behind the Roman and medieval walls was a bank, hence the rough inner face **C**. The circuit of the medieval wall is, not unnaturally, that of the Roman one and the medieval gates may also have replaced Roman ones. The Southgate at **D**, for example, seems to have incorporated part of a Roman structure.

The absence of a keystone in its arch is also said to indicate a Roman date although the castle's Norman gateway **8** does not have one either. ▶

▲ The city wall had few towers but along the length adjoining the Bishop's Close were two. This one, originally built in the thirteenth century and three storeys high, served as the Bishop's prison. The postern **A** was made in 1623. The tower and adjacent wall were extensively repaired in 1912.

◀ The two towers next to the Bishop's Close and this one at the eastern corner of the city reflect the absence of natural defences on this side. Everywhere else the wall followed the top of a natural slope **10A** or cliff **3B** and needed little extra protection. Here a ditch was added as well as the towers. From the greatly patched corner tower the wall ran to the Eastgate formerly at **A**, and onto the castle. The wall survived at **B** until destroyed by bombing in 1942. Its course is now marked in the flagstones and beneath it can be seen the passage or aqueduct which supplied water to the cathedral area.

The site of the castle is said to have been chosen by William the Conqueror himself. An L-shaped rampart and ditch **A**, as at Lydford, cut off the northern corner of the Roman wall and enclosed a small, natural, red hill — the *Rouge mont*. The stone gatetower must have been built soon after William's visit for the windows **B** are in 'Saxon' style as are the quoins at **C**. The sides with their pilasters **D** show no provision for attaching a stone curtain wall: the first earth and timber defences butted against the tower. In front of the rampart was a ditch with a bridge leading to the outer bailey. Both the latter and the bridge were captured by Stephen during his seige of 1136. ▶

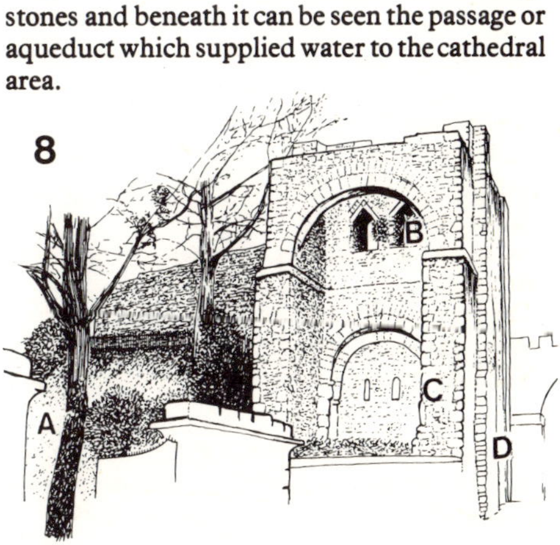

As the castle was built in a corner of the Roman defences there was the problem of sealing it from the existing city wall at **A**. This was done by tower **B**, which was probably in existence by 1136, for by then the timber walls had been replaced in stone and the pilasters, like those of the gateway **8D**, are characteristically Norman. The crenellation and turret **C** are, however, later.

9

From the hill occupied by the castle the city wall ran south-westwards along the edge of a valley, the steep slopes of which **A** provided defence. The valley also made communications difficult and the Northgate was but a minor one. In the nineteenth century the wall west of that gate was replaced by mausoleums or 'catacombs', eg **B**.

10

11

As early as 1160 there was a Guildhall, although the medieval parts of the present structure are later. The front was added in 1593 and described by a contemporary, Pole, as 'newe built very faire'. The building reflects the prosperity of the medieval city, which was large enough to have suburbs beyond the walls. That west of the river was served by St Thomas' church **1** and the fifteenth-century (manor) house at Bowhill, currently being conserved, was probably on its fringe.

12

▲ Within the city were sixteen parish churches, four religious houses such as St Nicholas' Priory and a number of almshouses like this one. The niche **A** probably contained a statue of the patron saint, St Catherine, and the buildings were ranged around a courtyard **B**.

13

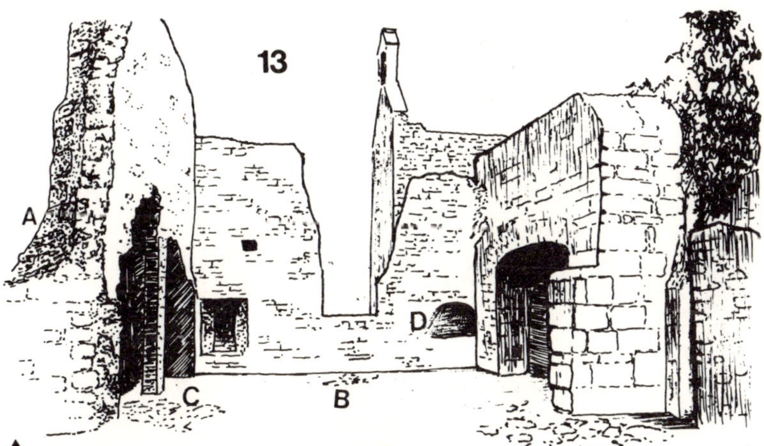


▲ The 'houses' had an upper floor reached by staircase **A** and, apparently a communal kitchen **B**. Fireplace **C** has an oven on the left-hand side, while another can be seen at **D**.

14

The chapel which was later converted had a ▶ piscina **A** and holy water stoup **B**.

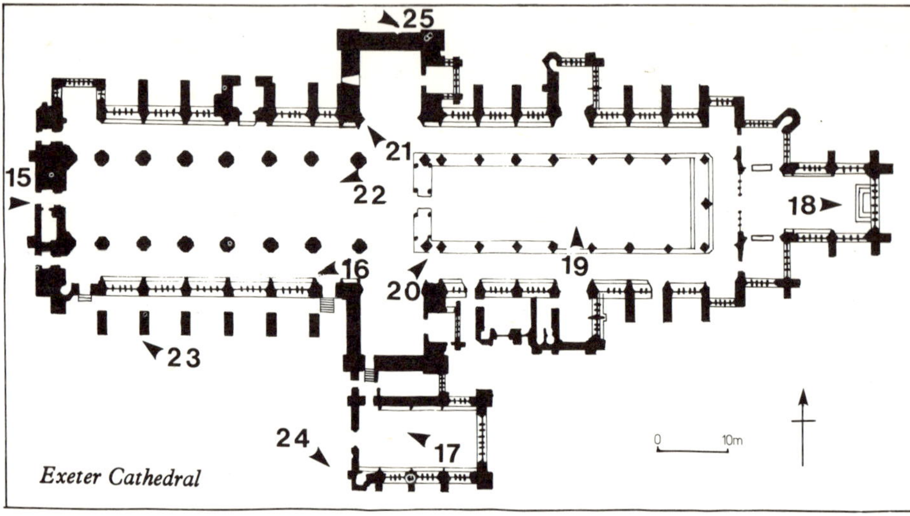


*Exeter Cathedral*

15

▲ The cathedral was built just beyond the eastern corner of the Roman *forum* — the public building at the centre of every Roman city. Excavation revealed that the *forum* had been built over the top of, and incorporated fragments of, a legionary bathhouse, for the city was preceded by a legionary fortress. Built in AD 55-60 and abandoned about AD 75 the fortress was probably the sourthern terminus of the road now called the Fosse Way. The Romans called the place *Isca*, a Latin rendering of the Celtic word for water — the fortress was probably a supply base provisioned by sea and river. After AD 75, with the advance of the Roman Army far to the north and the emergence of a civilian zone in the south, the site was laid out as the *Civitas* capital for the *Dumnonii* — the tribe which occupied an area comparable to that of modern Devon and Cornwall. The eastern corner of the old fortress had stood a little beyond the eastern end of the cathedral, but when the walls of *Isca Dumnoniorum* were later built they enclosed an area more than twice that of the military site.

A population seems to have survived within the walls for centuries after the Roman 'withdrawal'. By 926 the population of the city was mixed, for in that year William of Malmesbury records that Athelstan attacked the British 'with great energy, compelling them to withdraw from Exeter, which until that time they had inhabited on a footing of legal equality with the English. He then fixed the left bank of the Tamar as the ... boundary ... Having cleansed the city of its defilement by wiping out that filthy race, he fortified it ....'

Beyond the Tamar Athelstan created a British diocese based on St Germans. In 1043 Cornwall was absorbed into the diocese of Crediton, and when Leofric became bishop there in 1050 the centre was moved to Exeter. Leofric's cathedral was the church of St Mary and St Peter which stood on the site of the later St Mary Major at **A**. That church remained the cathedral until the new Norman one was ready for use in 1133.

16

▲

Apart from the two great towers, only fragments of the Norman cathedral survive. The alternately coloured stonework **A** and **B**, which clearly once flanked pillars, is usually attributed to that structure. Certainly it is earlier than the early fourteenth-century pillars **C** and **D**, but the lost pillars **A** and **B** cannot have supported a vault the width of the present aisle, as sometimes claimed, for a vault usually had the pillars at the corners of a square and the distance between **A** and **B** is shorter than the width of the aisle. It is possible, therefore, that pillars **A** and **B** belonged to an arcade. It is more likely, however, that the wall is a Norman addition for similar stonework occurs at Torre Abbey **6 A** and Exe Bridge **1** dating from about 1190. Such an explanation implies that the body of the Norman building was, until the construction of the 1190 wall, narrower than its successor and that the towers stood at the ends of the transepts. This would explain why the towers had to be broken into when the new (wider) building was begun. The old structure would be similar to the unknown building shown on the Common Seal of the City dated to 1170-80:

16a

◀

In 1225 Bishop Brewer gave an area of his garden 'sufficient...for making a chapter house'. The arcading **A** and doorway **B** are in early thirteenth-century style, so arch **C** must belong to Brewer's 'garden'. The upper part of the walls is in fifteenth-century style, indicating a rebuilding at that time. The new work may have been to allow the insertion of larger windows, or it may have followed structural damage by fire. ▶

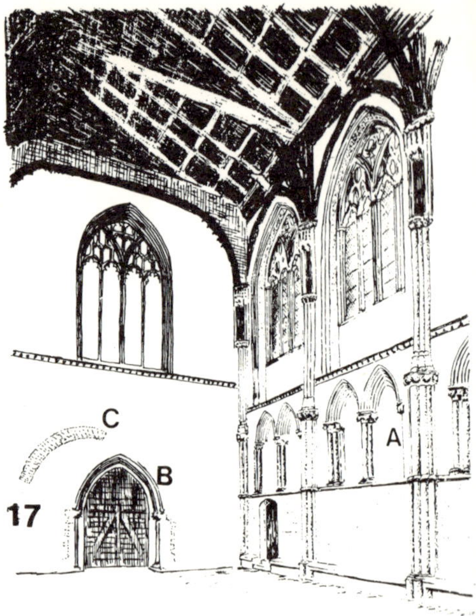


17

In the middle of the thirteenth century Bishop Bronscombe began to rebuild the whole of the cathedral in the new style of the chapter house **17A**. The work began to the east of the Norman cathedral with the construction of this Lady Chapel, the two flanking chapels, the outer wall and the chapels of St Andrew, St James and St Edmund. On 20 July 1280 Bronscombe wrote of the 'nearly completed new chapel next to the chapel of the Blessed Mary...on the south side where we have chosen our place of burial'. Two days later he died and was buried where he wished and where his tomb, with its later canopy, can still be seen. Bishop Quinil completed the chapels although the lead was not laid until 1303. The window tracery is attributed to him, as are the central bays of the reredos **A**, piscina **B** and sedilia **C**. Door **D** was cut in 1436 for a new vestry.

▼

18

19

▲
When the presbytery was begun in 1291 a more complex pillar than that used by Bronscombe was adopted (and used for the remainder of the building). The presbytery was completed in 1291 and painted in 1303. Its construction would have involved demolition of the Norman apse if that had not already occurred. That part of the apse may have been standing for a while within the shell of the new work, is suggested by the subtle differences between the choir **A** and presbytery **B**. The triforium at **C** and **D**, for example, is of different depths. The choir must, however, have been substantially complete by 1310 when Master John of Glaston was paid 52s 6d for moving the stalls to their new positions.

20

▶
The new choir was divided from the rest of the church by a screen **A**. Previous to 1310 the choir had extended into the nave, as was usual, and a similar screen or *pulpitum* there divided the religious from the populace. The narrow arch and bay **B** was caused by the need to put a pillar opposite each corner of the thick wall of the Norman towers. The use of two pillars, instead of one, suggests that the builders did not appreciate the problems of linking the Norman work to the new.

21

▲
When the nave was rebuilt the problem was partly solved by overlapping window **A** with the old wall — hence the stone work at **B** — and by making a longer bay than usual. The old towers had, however, been transformed into transepts in 1280 when Quinil had the walls, eg at **C** 'thrown down' and the large window **D** opened. The early date for the work is the reason why the supporting pillars, eg **E**, are — like their contemporaries in the Lady Chapel — simpler than elsewhere.

22

The pillars of the new nave were provided with ▶ a unique feature — seats **A**. The use of volcanic stone between the ribs of the vault **B** and not the sandstone used everywhere else suggests that it was intended to plaster between the ribs. This does not seem to have been done and the intention have may have been a victim of the Black Death in 1347-8. A result of the Death was a shortage of money and labour. When work was halted not all the windows had been glazed, so in 1350 ten men were hired to close them with wattle and daub to prevent the entry of birds. 450 loads of clay and 32 loads of twigs together with hay were needed.

At about the same time the cloisters were ▶ cleaned. Most of the cloisters were destroyed during Cromwell's rule, but traces of the arcading **A** can be seen. They seem to have been built about 1376-82 when rope for measuring and parchment for drawing the designs were bought. A marble floor was added in 1398 and the library area glazed in 1408-9.

23

24

▲
The present library building **A** and short length of cloister **B** are, however, nineteenth century although built on the site of the medieval structures.

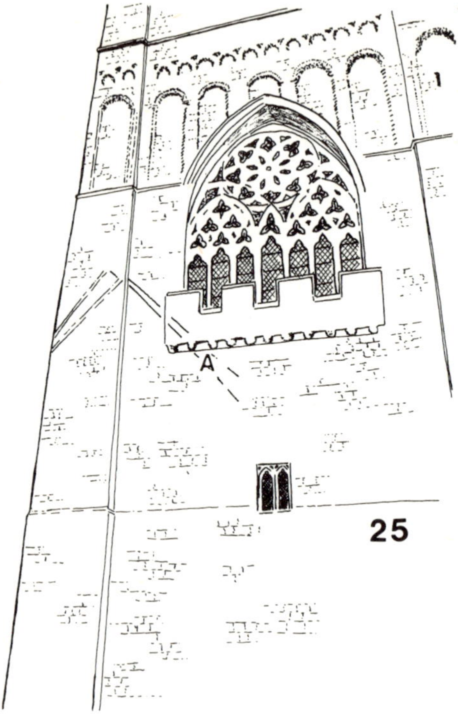


◀ The roof which joined the tower at **A** is that of the Treasurer's house built in 1402-3 and pulled down about 1820.

*The Roman city which replaced a legionary fortress was the capital for most of what is now Devon and Cornwall. Its wall – utilised by those who came after – took in a natural hill at one corner and that was later utilised by the Normans for a castle. In the tenth century Athelstan expelled the Britons and one hundred years later Leofric made it the ecclesiastical centre for Devon and Cornwall.*

**35 HEMBURY**
ST 101030

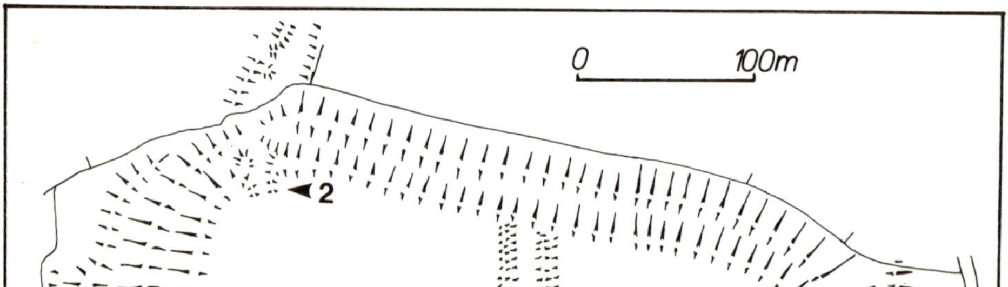

1

▲ The hillfort is located on the end of a spur and defended by a number of ramparts **A** and **B**. This form of rampart, essentially a steep slope, is known as *glacis*. The original profile of the hilltop remains at **C**, indicating that rampart **B** was constructed with material from ditch **D** and that the latter is largely a scraping of the hillside.

The ditches have now partly silted up and would originally have been deeper, but the effectiveness of the defences can be judged by trying to walk across them. Originally, with nothing other than perhaps grass to hold onto, they would have been very difficult to climb. ▼

1a

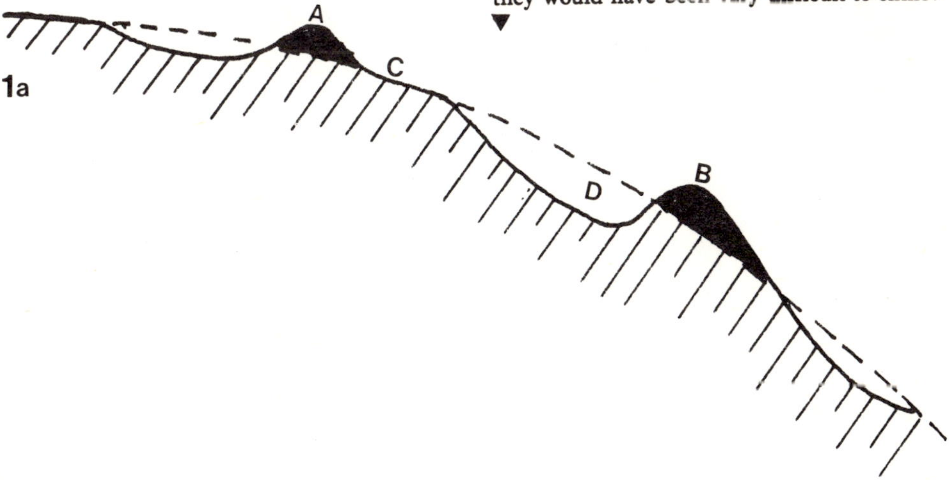

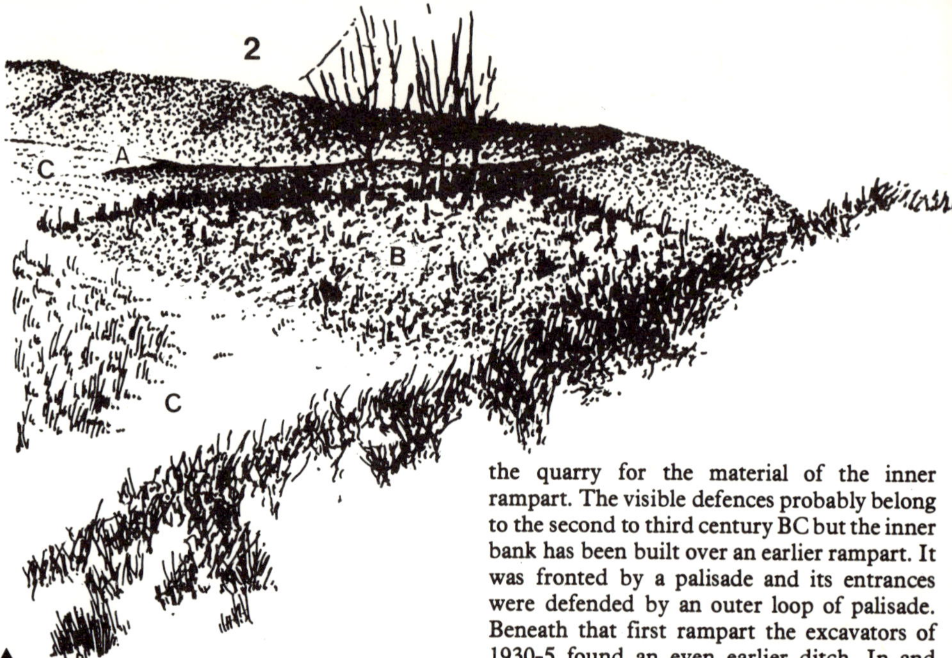


▲
There were two entrances with this one, perhaps, the more intact. The ends of the rampart were inturned **A** and **B**, to form a barbican-like passage with gates at the inner end. Any enemy who succeeded in forcing the passage would be halted by the gates and underfire from the sides. The slight hollow **C** is the quarry for the material of the inner rampart. The visible defences probably belong to the second to third century BC but the inner bank has been built over an earlier rampart. It was fronted by a palisade and its entrances were defended by an outer loop of palisade. Beneath that first rampart the excavators of 1930-5 found an even earlier ditch. In and behind it was Neolithic material. More recent excavations have also revealed a group of rectangular buildings associated with early Roman pottery, and it may be that a detachment of Roman troops was quartered inside the defences for a short period during the 'conquest'.

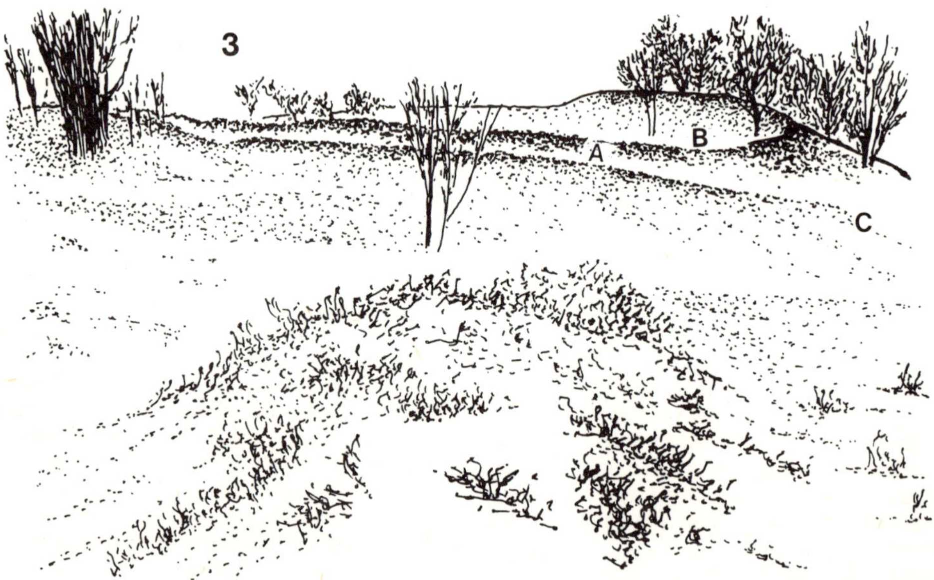

▲ The inturned end of rampart **A** shows that path **B** is the descendant of the Iron Age approach track.

Banks **A** and **B** may be the remains of fields contemporary with track **4B**. ▼

*The hillfort was built on the site of a Neolithic enclosure. It seems to have formed part of a landscape of fields and tracks.*

◀ The 1930s excavations uncovered a second Stone Age ditch beneath and behind the curious double bank **A**. The ditch had been dug as several short lengths each separated by a causeway. The feature was possibly only a quarry (or several quarries) for a continuous bank, but the hollows had been deliberately infilled with contemporary 'rubbish' not long after digging. The rectangular hut and fencing found at **B** also seems to have been contemporary. The remains suggest a Neolithic hilltop enclosure of the type archaeologists call causewayed camps. As the distinctive pottery had been brought some distance to the hilltop the site may have been a gathering place combining religion, market and fair. Gathering places certainly existed in later times and those north of Hadrian's Wall were called *loci* by the Romans. At least two can be recognised west of Exeter. The first, probably, St Michael's Mount, is the island described by pre-Roman geographers as the place where foreign merchants acquired tin. The second, not now identifiable, occurs as a Roman place name; Nemetostatio —*Nimet*, a sacred grove, and *Statio*, a tax centre. By coincidence Hembury was a fair-ground in more recent times, and double bank **A** may be related for it has been found to contain some relatively modern objects as well as late Iron Age ones. It is possible that the construction of **A** damaged the Iron Age entrance at **C**. Originally it may have had inturned ends like **2B** and **2C**.

## 36 Dunkeswell Abbey

ST 142107

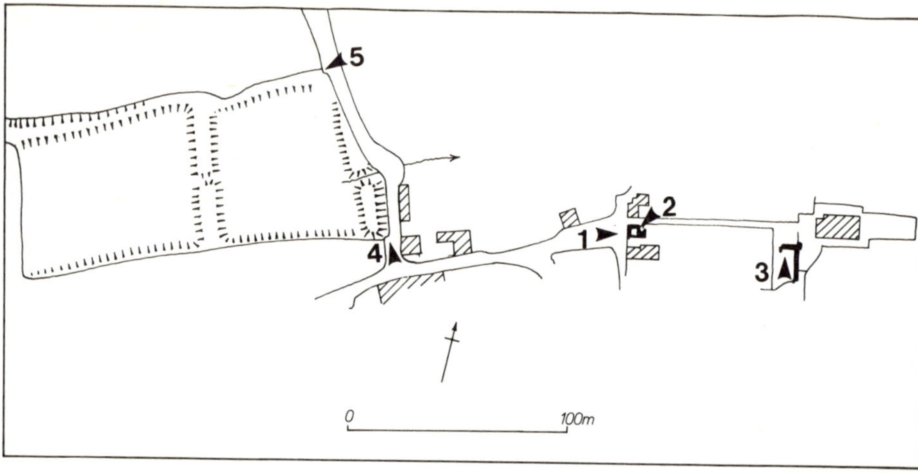


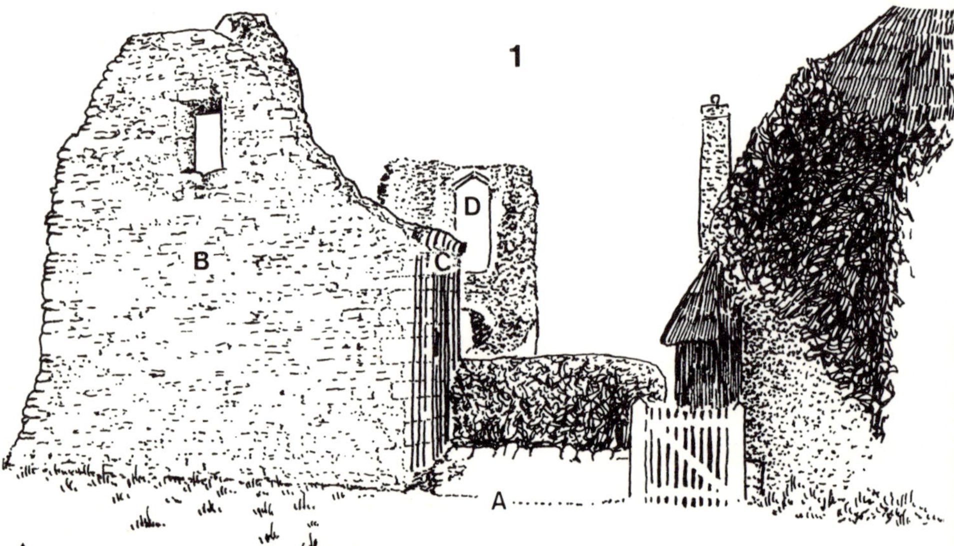


▲
The abbey, founded in the thirteenth century, consisted of conventual buildings around cloisters and a walled outer court. The latter was entered through this gatehouse, which seems to have been roughly symmetrical, passageway **A** being flanked by rooms like those at **B**. (The remains of the others were incorporated into the cottage.) The fragment of the arched portal **C** is in fifteenth-century style as is door **D**. It was usual to have accommodation for guests in the gatehouse and **D** may have led to another range.

◀ D is unlikely to have been for a staircase as one existed at **A**. The absence of external ground floor windows must have ensured privacy.

The principal remains of the conventual buildings are this gable wall with its steeply pitched roof **A**. The chimney **B** and oven **C** suggest that the ground floor was a kitchen, and as excavations in 1913 indicate that it formed the western side of the cloisters it was probably the refectory of the lay brethren — in a Cistercian abbey like this the lay brethren had their own accommodation on the western side of the cloisters. Nevertheless the excavations revealed that the conventual buildings possessed an unusual plan: the cloisters were elongated and not square and this western range projected beyond the end of the church. The lean-to roof **D** must represent use of the ruins.
▼

▶

2

3

▲
While the choir monks worked in the church and cloisters the lay brethren farmed the land around. Earthworks **A** and lane **B** may have been part of their fields. The stream was dammed **C** to form a fish pond.

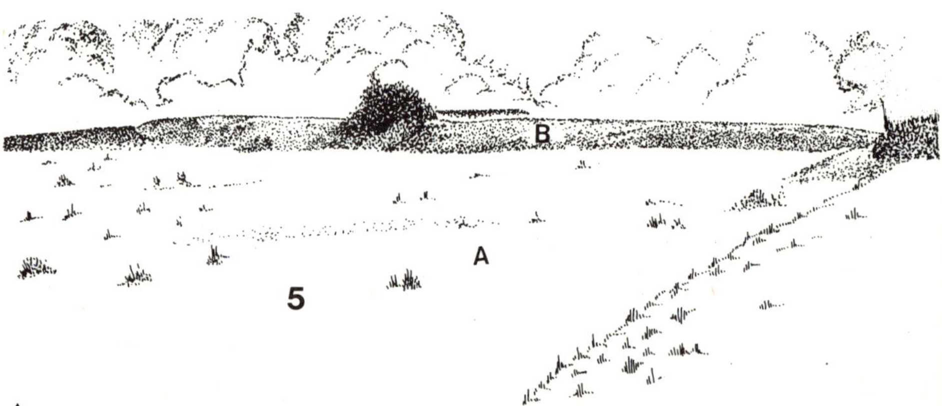


▲
Beyond that fishpond **A** was a second, behind dam **B**. Fish were important to the monks for monastic vows prohibited red flesh and fish could easily be kept throughout winter.

*This seems to have been a small Cistercian house with a slightly odd plan. As usual, however, the land around was farmed and there were also fishponds.*

# Glossary

*Apse* Semicircular end of a building or space.

*Bailey* Courtyard surrounded by a defensive perimeter.

*Barbican* Projection (normally in front of) a gateway, the idea being to allow defenders on its walls to fire at the back of the enemy trying to break down the main gate.

*Bay* Structural division of a roof, normally the area between pillars.

*Beaker* The distinctive pottery which appeared throughout much of Europe at the end of the third millenium BC. The people with whom it was associated (Beaker folk) were of different build and stature to the indigenous population. Associated with them is the earliest metal in Britain.

*beaker*

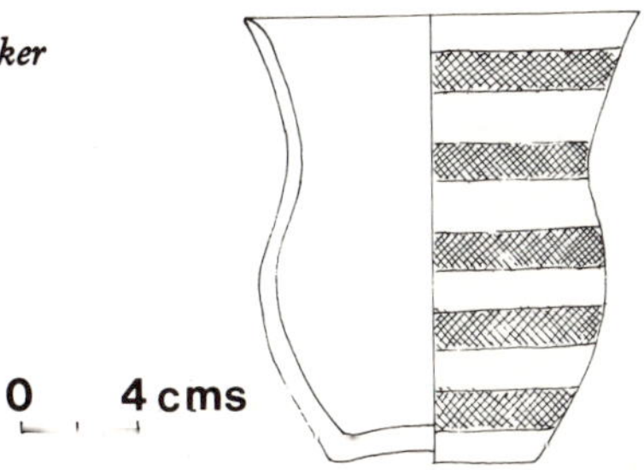


*Bronze Age* This loose and somewhat outdated term is applied to that period between approximately 2,000 BC and 800 BC.

*Butt Joint* A wall derives much of its strength from having the vertical joints overlapping. When two lengths of wall have been butted against each other because they were built at different times a single vertical joint often results.

*butt joint*

*Choir monks* Those whose principal duties were literary and worship. The manual jobs were often undertaken by largely illiterate members; the lay-brethren.

*Cist* Box-like arrangement of stones, usually for burial.

*Civitas* Roman administrative unit based (usually) on a tribal area with its city.

*Clerestory* The row of windows above the aisle roof which lit the central area directly.

*Conventual* Belonging to the convent — in its original sense the community, whether male or female.

*Curtain Wall* The perimeter wall between two towers.

*Dais* Raised platform for a table.

*Draw Bar* Doors were often secured by a horizontal baulk of timber, usually removed by sliding into a hole in the adjacent wall.

*Entablature* Frieze above a column or collonade.

*Fogou* Cornish name for a souterrain: an underground chamber or gallery.

*Garderobe* Latrine, often at the end of a passage or recess in the wall.

*Hood* Projection over a fireplace.

*hood*

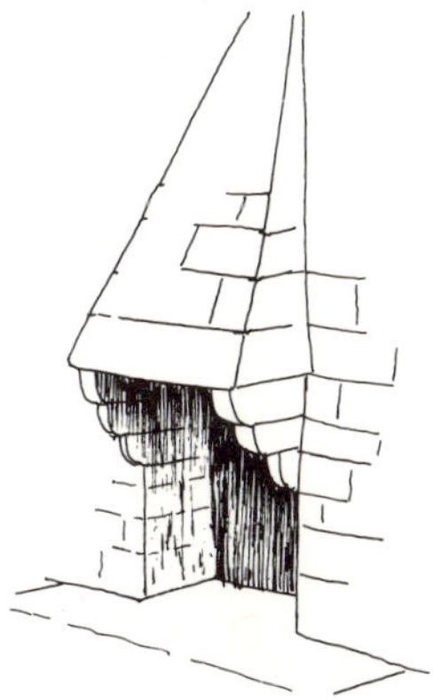

*Jamb* Side post of a doorway.

*Lancet* Early thirteenth-century style of window, narrow with a pointed head.

*Lay brethren* See choir monks.

*Loggia* Gallery or arcade, with one side open.

*Machicolation* Construction of the battlements well forward of the rest of the wall, allowing the defender behind to drop missiles through the parapet floor.

*machiolation*

*Motte* Large conical mound.
*Mullion* Vertical bar in a window.
*Nave* Western part of the church.
*Neolithic* New Stone Age, approximately 4,200-2,000 BC.
*Orthostat* Large slab set on edge to form a wall.
*Padstone* Stone on which a post was stood, either to spread the load and stop the upright sinking into the ground, or to act as a primitive damp course to prevent decay of the post.
*Pilaster* Square column like a shallow buttress.
*Piscina* Small basin with a drain beside an altar for washing sacramental vessels.
*Plinth* Projection of a wall ground level.
*Quoin* Corner stone.
*Radiocarbon Date* All living bodies absor and maintain a minute reservoir of radio activity. When the body dies the radio-activ material begins to decay at a fixed rate Measuring the proportion left within an objec allows the date when the object ceased to live t be established. However, a radiocarbon year i longer (by an uncertain amount) than calendar one. Hence an object 4,000 radio carbon years old is really more than 4,000 year old. To differentiate the two, BC is used t indicate calendar years and bc radiocarbo years. By the Neolithic the error is perhap about 10%.
*Reave* Bank or wall running across country apparently forming a boundary.
*Reredos* Decorated screen behind an altar
*Revett* Face, support, retain.
*Ringwork* Curvilinear, earthern rampart. Often circular.
*Scriptorium* Area where books were writter or copied.
*Sedilia* Seats for officiating priests.
*Slype* Passage.
*Solar* Upper room, lord's private area.
*Transepts* The arms of a cross shaped church.
*Triforium* Gallery between the main arches and the clerestory.

# Index